Advanced Reiki Healing

Enhance Your Skills in Reiki Healing,
Symbol Activations, Distance Healing,
Angelic Reiki, Crystal Healing, and More

Your Free Gift (only available for a limited time)

Thanks for getting this book! If you want to learn more about various spirituality topics, then join Mari Silva's community and get a free guided meditation MP3 for awakening your third eye. This guided meditation mp3 is designed to open and strengthen ones third eye so you can experience a higher state of consciousness. Simply visit the link below the image to get started.

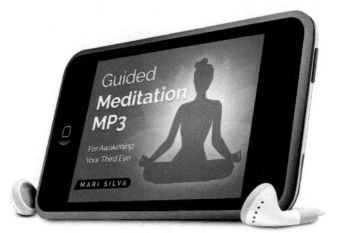

https://spiritualityspot.com/meditation

Contents

Introduction

In 1938, Madam Hawayo Takata brought the practice of Reiki to the west. Her journey brought one of the most beautiful fields of holistic healing a bit closer to us all. Since you are reading this, it probably isn't the first time you hear of Reiki. At the very least, you may have heard it from someone in passing or stumbled across it on the internet. Or you've received your first attunement and are well on your way to starting your second-degree Reiki class. You've probably decided to read all you can to improve on your knowledge of Reiki as a form of alternative medicine.

Whatever stage you are in on your Reiki journey, in this book, you will learn Reiki history, rules, and what to expect if you make Reiki your field of expertise.

When was the last time you read a text that addressed all the burning questions you had about Reiki as a holistic healing modality? Well, if there's one thing you should know about this book, it's this: You are about to take a deep dive into the most important things you will need to know about Reiki.

Holistic medicine is a remedy for the mind, body, and soul. I mention this because you must know Reiki is not a cure; neither is it a substitute for orthodox treatment. Reiki is divine boundless energy used to alleviate deep-seated malaise present in both the body and the mind.

Alternative medicine, particularly Reiki, is in more demand today than ever before due to a host of reasons, one of them being the rising cost of healthcare.

What if I told you that you could heal yourself? What if there is an approach that creates harmony between the mind, soul, and body? What would you do if you discovered you are a channel for high natural healing vibrations that can help not just you, but countless others as well?

All these topics and more are subjects we will explore in this book. I urge you to suspend your beliefs and consider the information here as a guide to the universal energy that is Reiki. I wish you love, light, and happiness in your journey to self-healing!

Chapter One: The Three Pillars of Reiki: Gassho, Reiji-Ho, and Chiryo

A Brief Background of Reiki

Reiki is a form of alternative medicine commonly known as energy healing. Reiki masters use a hands-on healing approach through which universal energy or "Qi" transfers from the palms of the master to the body of the patient to accelerate physical or emotional healing. In scholarly texts or journals, it is regarded as a pseudoscience, as there is no definitive proof or irrefutable evidence that "a universal life force" exists, but you already know there are things beyond the realm of orthodox science.

The Oxford English dictionary breaks down the etymology of the Japanese word Reiki. Rei means "soul" or "spirit," while Ki means "energy," "life force," or "Consciousness." The earliest use of the word Reiki in English texts was in 1975. It embraces all religious practices and affiliations. It is merely a subtle yet efficient way of channeling life force for healing and general well-being. Its masters understand that everyone can connect with their vital life force, which should ideally be firm and unrestrained in a healthy state. Illness happens because of weak, blocked, or unbalanced Ki.

Inception and Rediscovery

Recent history considers Mikao Usui or Usui Sensei to be the father of Reiki. This reason is why, in many texts, the word only applies to the holistic healing he developed. Historians beg to differ. The book "An Evidence-Based History of Reiki" by Toshitaka Mochitzuki Sensei and Hiroshi Doi Sensei, two Reiki researchers, shows that before healing methods developed by Usui Sensei, there were at least four other Reiki methods practiced in early Japan. Among them are Reisen Oyama's Seido Reisho-Jutsu, Reikan Tonetsu Ryoho, founded by Ishinuki Reikaku, and Senshin-Ryu Reiki Ryoho founded by Matsubara Kogetsu.

Usui Sensei himself never called his method of holistic healing Reiki, as he chose the phrase Shin-shin Kai-Zen Usui Reiki Ryoho, which means "the Usui- Reiki treatment method for the mind and body improvement." We call this Usui Reiki Ryoho, as it's less of a mouthful. Usui Sensei understood his take on Reiki, while valid, wasn't the only one.

Reiki energy has existed for about 2,500 years and was said to have originated in Tibet. The Tibetan Lamas learned to harness the life force of vitality and self-preservation encoded in human nature for insight, healing, and overall well-being, and spiritual guidance. It is known by different names, as Prana by Hindus, the Holy Spirit by Christians, Ki by the Japanese, and Chi by the Chinese.

This profound knowledge of Reiki was closely guarded and only passed on by word of mouth to those deemed worthy of the knowledge, who had devoted time and energy to the spiritual practice of experiencing harmony of body and spirit.

There isn't much information available on Reiki history because at the end of the Second World War, the Japanese had no choice but to surrender totally to the US government. The government enacted laws banning all Eastern healing methods and endorsed Orthodox healing practices. Some Eastern healers, like the acupuncturists, could continue practicing. Still, practitioners of Usui Reiki Ryoho Gakkai went against the US government licensing regulations to become a secret society, practicing only in private meetings and discussing Reiki with a select few members of their Gakkai group.

The most comprehensive information on Reiki history comes from the Gakkai. This is probably because the first president of the group was none other than Usui Sensei himself, his successors being Shihans or Reiki masters, personally trained by Usui and authorized to pass on the knowledge of the practice in his absence.

A thorough understanding of the Usui Reiki system is crucial since it provides practitioners with a solid foundation for understanding Reiki healing, making it easier for them to connect with its essence. While other methods have faded into oblivion, this one has stood the test of time because of Hawayo Hiromi Takata, a Reiki Grandmaster trained by Chujiro Hayashi, a naval physician, and disciple of Mikao Usui. Hayashi was one of the key players in demystifying Reiki and aiding its transmission out of Japan. Madam Takata brought Reiki to the West, where it became the most practiced form in the world.

The Spread of Reiki in the West

Mikao Usui was born on the 15th of August 1865 in Taniai village, Miyama-Cho district of Gifu prefecture, Japan, where his ancestors lived for 11 generations. His family was Buddhist. Young Mikao was sent off by his parents to a Tendai monastery for his primary education. Later in 1888, Usui suffered cholera during an epidemic in Kyoto. His illness resulted in a near-death experience where he claimed to have received visions from Buddha. These visions led to him developing more than just a keen interest in the science of healing.

Usui Sensei spent a lot of time and money in his spiritual pursuits. After 21 days of fasting, meditation, and prayers in a cave on mount Kurama, he attained the state of An-shin Ritsu-mei. This state had evaded him for years, but after fasting for three weeks, Mikao Usui received a vision that forever altered his life. He saw ancient Sanskrit symbols that helped him develop his method of Reiki as we know it today.

Mikao Usui recounts seeing bubbles of light floating from the heavens. These bubbles descended from above into his body and left through his hands. He called those light bubbles Reiki. After his religious experience, he sustained an injury on his foot on his descent from the mountain. Usui Sensei placed his hands on his foot, and his wound healed miraculously. From then on, Mikao collected ancient Sanskrit texts and sutras from Buddhist monasteries and libraries abundant in Japan at the time to grasp the concept of Reiki in healing himself and others.

He soon became an advanced meditation master and esoteric healer, offering treatments to both rich and poor. His "medical generosity" didn't go down well with the typical class-oriented Japanese society. The entire family ostracized Usui, his name burnt off the ancestral register. Even his daughter Toshiko had a clause in her will stating that her father's name never is mentioned in her home.

Usui Sensei continued teaching and healing, eventually developing a close kinship with Watanabe Kioshi, his Buddhist teacher's son. Watanabe became not only his dearest friend, but his most devout student. In April 1922, Usui Sensei moved to Tokyo and founded the Usui Reiki healing method society, where he taught classes and ran a healing clinic. He had many students. The most notable of them were Chujiro Hayashi (who later became the second Reiki Grandmaster) and Toshihiro Eguchi.

In some traditional Reiki stories, Usui Sensei was a lecturer at the Doshisha University of Kyoto. He then traveled to the United States, where he lived for seven years, receiving his doctorate in theology from the University of Chicago Divinity School. It is important to refute this falsehood. Usui may have been fascinated by all things Western; still, there is evidence to prove there are no records of him as a lecturer or student in either Doshisha University or the University of Chicago.

Reiki Master William Rand discovered these findings and observed that these theories in Reiki history were created to make Reiki's power acceptable to the Westerners. At the peak of early Reiki history, Usui Sensei urged Hayashi to open a Reiki clinic based on his experience as a naval physician. Soon, Hayashi Reiki Kenkyukai Institute, a school that doubled as a clinic, was born. Mikao Usui died of a stroke on the 9th of March 1926, at the age of 62. Before he died, he gave his class notes, sacred Buddhist texts, and diary — all in a lacquered box — to his friend Watanabe.

Hayashi tweaked Usui's methods for optimum effect. Where Usui had each patient seated to receive treatment from one Reiki practitioner at a time, Hayashi Sensei instructed the patient to lie down to receive treatment from multiple Reiki practitioners at once. Hawayo Takata, the third Reiki Grandmaster, is credited with its spread and its precepts as we know them today.

Hawayo Takata was a Japanese American born in Hawaii in 1990, widowed 30 years later, and left to fend for two kids. She worked tirelessly. Five years later, her job's stress took its toll, leaving her with a lung infection and abdominal pain.

A hospital in Japan diagnosed her with appendicitis, gallstones, a tumor, and asthma. As if that wasn't enough, she suffered a nervous breakdown. She was asked to prepare for surgery, but her respiratory distress put her at the risk of death following anesthesia. Her physician told her of Hayashi Sensei's clinic, and she gave it a try.

After four months of twice-daily Reiki treatments, Hawayo was healed. She took her belief in Reiki to another level, learning it and becoming a Grandmaster. She didn't stop there. Hawayo taught no less than 22 masters to carry on her teachings. The role of Hawayo is essential to Reiki not only because of her part in preserving Reiki culture but also because she was the first female Reiki student. Originally, Reiki was an art taught only to men in Japanese society.

In the United States alone, Reiki therapy is accepted as an unorthodox form of treatment by the National Center for Complementary and Alternative Medicine. It is available at medical spas and high-end health resorts for stress relief, pain reduction, pre- and post-operative therapy for cancer patients, and so on. Thanks to Hawayo and other dedicated students of the Usui Reiki system, Reiki has become a tested and trusted holistic therapy method worldwide.

The Five Principles

There are five principles or ideals of Reiki, which you are supposed to understand as a practitioner. These principles are not hard-and-fast rules that govern the way you live, but are simply guidelines or precepts that help bring balance and harmony to your life. The more you work within the framework of these principles, the more they become second nature.

When practicing the principles, always remember your human nature. When you stumble or falter in any of the steps, it's okay to try again tomorrow. These principles are:

- Just for today, I will let go of anger.

- Just for today, I will not worry.

- Just for today, I will be grateful for my many blessings.

- Just for today, I will do my work honestly.

- Just for today, I will be kind to my neighbor and every other living being.

Now let's shed light on each principle and the importance of its application in our daily lives.

Releasing Angry Thoughts: When was the last time something or someone made your blood boil? Does it irritate you when life moves slower than you expect? Anger is more than an emotion. Anger is energy. The root cause of anger can be simplified into a lack of control. Whether this lack of control concerns circumstances in your life or people's treatment of you, the need to lash out is normal and sometimes even necessary. The first principle teaches that even though it is alright to get mad, you can manage your reactions by practicing patience, tolerance, and acceptance.

Letting Go of Worry: Worry does nothing for you. It keeps you in a troubled state of mind, and possibly, leads you to take actions that will only exacerbate whatever troublesome situation you're concerned about. Learn to let go of the things you cannot control and simply allow the chips to fall where they may. There's no power in worry, which means there's no point letting it consume you.

Fear creates tension, which messes you up physically by weakening your immune system, and emotionally, by feeding all the shame and regret. It may seem that you're worried because of things outside of you, but the truth is worry comes from within. Even in Ayurveda, the third or solar plexus chakra is known as the source of fear, while the fifth or throat chakra is the seat of anxiety. Reiki teaches the power of breath to banish fear and worry in your daily life.

The Peace You Find with Gratitude: Have you ever just looked at something or someone and felt thankful? It is easy to feel grateful for those warm and fuzzy days. Gratitude means being thankful for the clouds, the thunder, and the rain. Look at it this way: Without one, you cannot appreciate the other.

Gratitude is a powerful emotion and an excellent motivator. Life is challenging, forcing you to move like a cat on hot bricks. Instead of concentrating on the pain on the soles of your feet, why not pretend you are tap dancing? Reiki forces you to acknowledge the positive and negative. It relieves you of your worries and reminds you to remain in the present. Like Yin and Yang, both good and bad experiences help you on your journey to a more harmonious existence.

Developing Integrity: What is your word worth? If lawyers or contracts didn't exist, would your speech and a handshake prompt you to remain honest in your dealings with all and sundry? Would you bail if you had nothing or no one holding you back from specific responsibilities, whether it's the dishes in the sink or your business or personal dealings with others? Would you disclose something told to you in confidence by an ex-friend or lover because you had to make conversation?

Sometimes honesty and integrity can be confusing. Other times, they can conflict with the situation you find yourself in. Practicing Reiki helps you connect deeper with yourself and others. This way, you can decide with your head screwed on tight.

Practicing Kindness to Yourself and Others: The principle of kindness in Reiki is like Ahimsa's Yoga philosophy, which translates to "do no harm." Little wonder why it is contained in the Hippocratic oath, written in Latin as primum non nocere, which means "first, do no harm." Kindness need not be a grand gesture or donating your trust fund to charities in developing countries.

Kindness is in the little things, recognizing that everyone is unique, with belief systems and opinions that differ from your own. It is doing good without bias. It is an awareness and consideration for your surroundings, animals, plants, and others besides yourself. Kindness to oneself is also important. That's why affirmations are a thing, and confidence coaching is an actual job.

Kindness to self involves recognizing your fallibility and forgiving yourself, treating yourself when you feel like, and not shying away from a pick-me-up either from friends, Netflix, or Ben and Jerry's. Kindness to self means making time for you, honoring your dreams, setting boundaries, accepting, and believing in yourself. There are other ways to do this, but they are beyond the scope of this text. Reiki is practiced as a form of self-care and is used to heal emotional and physical wounds.

The Three Pillars

The pillars of Reiki are considered rituals that help strengthen a Reiki session, allowing the practitioner to develop a connection with their consciousness and the Reiki source. The Reiki ritual is broken down into three parts or pillars:

- Gassho
- Reiji-Ho
- Chiryo

They each have unique attributes and functions in preparing the practitioner to become a conduit for life force or Reiki energy when practiced in perfect synchronicity.

Gassho: This is the first pillar. The word Gassho means "two hands coming together," like the Hindu greeting Namaste, which literally means "I bow to you," but has a deeper spiritual meaning: "The God in me recognizes the God within you."

Gassho consists of breathing, centering, and meditation, all of which help funnel Reiki energy through you. Once you assume the Gassho position, calming and centering yourself with the recommended breathing techniques helps you set and strengthen your intentions for the healing session.

Practicing Gassho: The Gassho ritual helps focus and still the mind during meditation. Here's how to practice:

- Place your hands together in a prayer position, making sure your fingers touch tip to tip. Do not apply pressure. Ensure your fingertips are relaxed while in contact. You should only feel pressure on the middle fingers.

- While your hands are in Gassho's position, focus your thoughts on the point where your middle fingers meet and let your thoughts melt away like ice in the summer breeze.

- If your mind wanders as it is wont to do, apply pressure on the middle fingers, and try concentrating again.

- While in this state, ground yourself and become one with the earthly vibrations from mother nature. Recite the five Reiki principles aloud or silently in your mind for 15 to 30 mins.

- When done with meditation, end the session by setting an intention of gratitude.

The posture and meditation practice in this ritual are symbolic and beneficial. Sitting with the spine straight prevents our Reiki from getting clipped by slouching. The hand gesture is a mudra, a posture that allows us to generate and channel energy in specific ways to convey a spiritual meaning. The middle fingers also serve as a focal point of awareness during meditation.

Reiji-Ho: This is the second pillar. Reiji translates to "an indication of Reiki power," while Ho means "method." As the second pillar, it is the part where the practitioner asks for divine guidance. When in this state, request that the energy be turned on. After this, set an intention for the direction of Reiki power.

Practicing Reiji-Ho: Here's how you use it correctly:

- Keep your hands in the Gassho position, ensuring your wrists are close to, even touching, the center of your chest.

- With your eyes shut, ask for the Reiki life force to flow within your being. Pray or ask for the well-being of your patient.

- Raise your hands to touch your Ajna chakra (the third eye chakra between and slightly above the brows) and ask for guidance on where to direct the Reiki energy.

- While in this step, don't move your hands haphazardly. Allow your emotions to be guided. Like a stream of clear water, let your hands move with intention. Set your mind free from any desires regarding the outcome of the Reiki session.

- Now, allow your hands to hover relaxedly above your patient's body while you wait for guidance from Reiki energy. All you must do is trust the Reiki and the power of your intuition.

The ritual of Reiji-Ho allows you to connect with the universe intentionally, and the infinite power of love. This universal energy is always in motion. So, this step serves three purposes: It makes you aware of this cosmic life force, opens your mind for the flow of this energy, and helps direct energy toward your conscious intention.

Chiryo: Chiryo refers to "treatment." This is the final pillar of Reiki. In Chiryo, the practitioner leaves their ego at the doorstep, allowing themselves to become a channel or conduit for Reiki energy.

During this ritual, the practitioner places their dominant hand on the patient's Ajna chakra and waits until they receive a signal to proceed. The energy determines where the ailment resides and directs itself toward it. The practitioner uses intuition during hand placement while remaining guided by the life force to nourish and cleanse the patient's body until the end of the session. It is possible to perform Chiryo on yourself. Here's how:

- Get seated in a comfortable sitting or standing position and place your hands in Gassho. Shut your eyes and let go of fear and anxiety.

- Raise your hands, holding them up as high as you possibly can. With your hands raised, visualize the Reiki energy in the form of light rays spreading through your entire body. With this vision in mind, take a deep breath in.

• Breathe out. As you do, visualize the light which fills your body, spreading out all around you, in every possible direction. This breathing technique is called Joshin Kokyu-Ho. This technique helps strengthen your connection to Reiki, purifies the body and mind, and reduces tension. There are also testimonies that it increases intuitive abilities.

Chapter Two: The Three Degrees of Reiki

Usui Sensei divided his training into three levels. He called the first Shoden, which was further divided into four classes:

- Loku-Tou

- San-Tou

- Yon-Tou

- Go-Tou

The second degree is called inner teaching or Okuden, further subdivided into two levels:

- Okuden-Zen Ki

- Okuden Koe-Ki

The third degree or mystery teaching was called Shinpiden. This is the level also known as the mastery level in Western teachings. Shinpiden is taught in two stages:

- Shihan-Kaku (assistant teacher)

- Shihan (master teacher or venerable master)

First Degree

This is the entry-level where you are taught Reiki history, lineage, hand positions, Reiki self-healing, and so on. While studying Reiki lineage in some centers, you might be shown an organogram of sorts showing your connection to Usui Sensei through generations of Reiki teachers. Some teachers teach first degree alone, while others teach second-degree Reiki.

In Reiki I, you receive your first attunement. These attunements help open your energy channels so you can heal yourself, family members, or pets. After the attunement, there is a period of change and cleansing, just like a detox.

The attunement acts as a broom, clearing the cobwebs and minimizing blocked energy channels. This process might last for 21 days, a tribute to the number of days Usui Sensei spent on mount Kurama. During and after the spiritual detox, it would be wise to remain hydrated and get as much rest as you can manage.

Second Degree

This is an upgrade from the first degree. At this level, you have expressed your interest in becoming a Reiki practitioner. This is when you are taught the Reiki symbols. These symbols are an empowering and distinct feature of the practice. Three symbols are learned in the second degree, while the only one is taught in the third degree.

Apart from the symbols, you are taught how to design a healing session, the ethics of treating others, distance healing, and the importance of a code of honor in Reiki practice. You will not only learn to draw the symbols but to channel Reiki using them. The characters taught in the second degree are:

- Cho Ku Re — The power symbol

- Sei Hei Ki — The mental and emotional symbol

- Hon Sha Ze Sho Nen — The distance symbol

After completing second-degree Reiki, you become a Reiki practitioner.

Third Degree

This is the master level. Here you learn the art of becoming a Reiki master. You also learn how to teach Reiki and use the master level symbol known as Dai Ko Myo. Some other Reiki branches educate students on lesser-known characters such as Raku and the Tibetan fire symbol, also called Tibetan Dai Ko Myo or Domo.

The mastery level not only helps you gain all levels of attunement, but trains you to give attunement to others. Many centers advocate six months or more between the second and third degrees to integrate the principles from the earlier course before attempting the next class.

Reiki Symbols Demystified

Reiki symbols have been kept secret for generations. For many decades, they were never copied or printed. Students were forbidden to take their notes home or show them to others. In Hawayo Takata's class, students had to burn their notes after each lesson. This led to so many aspects of Reiki's symbolism becoming lost.

Just imagine being a teacher, and suddenly, you cannot remember the exact way a symbol is drawn. Because human memory is rarely perfect and for fear of misleading your students, what do you do? You skip teaching the hazy bits. Well, at a point in Reiki history, there were many variations of each symbol due to insufficient documentation.

History has it that initially, there were about 300 symbols, although only 22 are in use today. Besides the few taught in Reiki II and III, some remaining characters are kept ostentatiously hidden in Tibetan monasteries and libraries. I say "some," because the Chinese Communist Party has taken over Tibet, and the precious little knowledge left of Reiki is being systematically destroyed or diluted with Western knowledge. There are whispers that ancient Reiki texts were smuggled in by monks who migrated to India, but many ancient texts are lost to us forever.

Diane Stein's book "*Essential Reiki*" is a Reiki fan favorite. This text is a complete guide to demystifying Reiki symbolism, going against the traditional compulsion of secrecy to make these symbols public knowledge.

Just like you, there are many others thirsty for the knowledge of Reiki, but they lack the time to devote their existence to the sacred path. People argue that Stein's methods may land the symbols into the wrong hands and promote misuse. On that note, I would love to clear up some misconceptions about Reiki symbols.

What Reiki Is and Isn't

Reiki symbols are Sanskrit-derived Japanese letters as old as 2,500 years old. They are psychically drawn as pictures or chanted as mantras. The symbols are universal, unique, and a powerful aspect of Reiki that allows you to connect better with the limitless universal life force. Think of them as keys or switches that unlock or amplify Reiki energy.

Usui Sensei first taught Reiki without using symbols. After a while, he introduced the characters to help practitioners heighten their healing abilities. An integral aspect of studying Reiki; these symbols are said to bridge the gap between healer and patient, raise consciousness, activate self-healing abilities, and rid the mind of destructive thought patterns.

In general, symbols tap into more profound energy and consciousness that transcends worlds. Each symbol's power represents years of use in metaphysics and healing by thousands of teachers and practitioners.

The symbols were initially kept secret to keep them sacred and pure. This secrecy was encouraged because it was a means to maintain the symbols' power and keep the sacred connection, but the characters are only mere drawings without attunement.

Reiki is not belief, psychic healing, hypnosis, or mind control. Its goal is not to initiate dogma or affect your thinking process. It is not limited to hands-on healing. It is an energy form that could be used to heal across time and dimensions.

It isn't limited to healing illnesses. Daily practice fine-tunes the force field of your body, allowing it to act as a barrier to disease-causing organisms or processes. Like your daily glass of orange juice, a cup of coffee, or a protein shake, it can serve as your daily supplement for wellbeing. It's not a massage either, although practitioners can combine it with massage therapy for optimum results.

When using Reiki symbols, the power of your intention supersedes the exact replication of the symbol. I say this because drawing characters could be tasking for newbies, so if you fall into this category, don't beat yourself up about it. Just make sure your intentions are pure, clear, and focused. The symbols cannot harm, regardless of your negative intentions. This is because its energy is a master of itself. It is purposeful, positive, and authentic. The symbols are only designed to conjure this pure energy.

It is possible to practice Reiki without symbols. This is done in some areas of Japan, and this form of initiation is called *Rejiu*. It doesn't drain you of energy. As a practitioner, you are an energy conduit attuned to nature's limitless energy supply.

Reiki Symbols

The first two Reiki symbols are derived from Shinto and Buddhist traditions, but they have assigned Japanese names or forms. The last two are Japanese kanji in Chinese characters.

Cho Ku Rei — The Symbol of Power

Cho Ku Rei is pronounced as Cho-coo-ray. It is the first and most flexible Reiki symbol. It is translated as "place all the power of the universe here, now." For this reason, Cho Ku Rei (CKR) is regarded as the activator, opener, light switch, or doorway to healing.

Many practitioners draw tiny Cho Ku Rei on their palms before beginning a healing session to activate Reiki energy. The symbol itself is not an energy storage unit. It represents your intention. Your objective activates the power. Drawing the characters is only a physical action that reinforces your intentions.

Drawing Cho Ku Rei

1. Draw a horizontal line from left to right. This represents a connection with the universal life force.

2. Draw another line, a vertical one, this time from top to bottom. It should join the horizontal line previously drawn. This line represents light flowing from the soul star chakra, the crown chakra, and the rest of the chakras.

3. Draw three and a half decreasing circles that finish on the vertical line. The seven intersections of these circles symbolize the seven primary chakras. When appropriately drawn, it should resemble something like this:

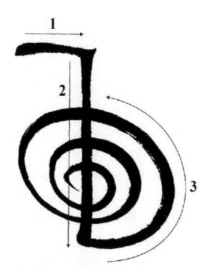

Diving Deeper into Cho Ku Rei

- The word Cho means "to sever." This rids the mind of illusions to perceive the whole.

- Ku means "to penetrate." Like a dagger, this symbol slices through dimensions.

- Rei means "omnipresence," "universality," or "the etheric level."

This symbol cuts through barriers of resistance. Esoterically, it means "dis-creation." The symbol activates second-degree energy. Without it, you are only channeling first-degree Reiki.

The spiral shape of the Reiki symbol is known as a labyrinth. In planetary archaeology, spirals represent the energy of the goddess, so the initiation spot at the Minoan Snake Goddess Temple in the Palace of Knossos on Crete has the labyrinth symbol.

CKR functions on the physical plane, concentrating Reiki on the focused spot using its sign's spiral shape. Its characteristic shape allows energy to swirl and focus on whichever direction you wish it to go. You may use it clockwise for the increase and counterclockwise for the decrease.

Traditionally, CKR is drawn counterclockwise from right to left. Still, many practitioners of metaphysics, alchemy, the healing arts, and even some sects like the Wiccans have observed that the symbol works for increase when drawn counterclockwise in the northern hemisphere.

Drawing it counterclockwise causes reduction or dispersion (the opposite goes for the southern hemisphere dwellers). If you find a particular direction works for you, no matter your hemisphere, use it consistently.

Many teachers only apply the counterclockwise CKR in cases of tumors, fevers, or cancers, as clockwise CKR only aggravates the condition while the opposite quells the spread or shrinks the growth. Double CKR, one drawn in each direction, are used mostly in manifestation.

Using CKR on Yourself

• You can draw the symbol on your non-dominant palm using your dominant hand and vice versa to help you focus and call forth Reiki energy. When you become an advanced student, you may not need to use symbols to conjure up this energy, as you will always be directly connected to it.

• You can draw CKR on your energy centers, namely the crown, throat, solar plexus, inguinal, and umbilical regions. The Reiki conjured can deeply cleanse them all.

• CKR can also work as a mood booster by reducing fatigue.

• When used on secondary energy centers such as the ears, eyes, shoulders, knees, pelvis, feet, and back, this symbol can create a shield that protects your aura from negative people and energy.

• Drawing this symbol on the pad of each finger can aid in deep cleansing your energy field and that of others. Some practitioners use this after self-treatment or treatment of others.

• You can ditch your sleeping pills in favor of CKR. Draw this symbol on all your energy centers, and along with mindful breathing, you will experience the best sleep of your life. Etching this symbol onto your bedding can help keep bad dreams at bay.

• If you feel soreness in a particular region of your body, draw this symbol on the palm of your hand and place it over the painful area for 5 to 10 minutes for optimum results.

• Are you scared? Anxious? Suffering from stage fright? Draw this symbol on the heels of your feet for extra grounding. When doing this, visualize a stronger anchor to the ground and watch as you gain that extra pep in your step. You can also engrave CKR on a tiger eye bracelet or stone to boost your confidence.

Using CKR on Others

There are six known ways to transfer the CKR symbol from yourself to a patient.

• Imagine a luminescent white CKR symbol projected from your Ajna chakra and focused onto the back of your palms while you rest them using different hand positions on your client.

• Draw the symbol using your tongue onto the roof of your mouth. Direct the energy from the sign to the back of your hands as they hover above your client's form.

• Imagine a brilliant light encompassing the symbol on the palm of your hands before placing them on your client.

- Draw the symbol on the roof of your mouth using your tongue. Project the same sign on the back of your palms before placing it on your client.

- You may also draw the symbol on your palms using your index finger before starting a session.

- Draw the symbol in the air using your index finger, stating the direction you want the Reiki to go. There is a caveat, though: allow no one to see you drawing this symbol, except they are a Reiki master or a second-degree Reiki initiate.

After transferring the symbol to your patient, activate them by silently chanting the words "Cho Ku Rei" three times. Note that the characters drawn will never work until this silent invocation.

Cho Ku Rei for Removing Blockages: When there is an energy block, the body's vibrations change. They could get cut off, become slow, or even worse, remain stagnant. These energy blocks are responsible for chronic illness and stress. For instance, when you use CKR on a bleed or a minor cut, you may notice the wound bleeds profusely. This is normal and only lasts briefly. It is Reiki forcing your body to harmonize energy flow. This effect will lead to accelerated healing.

CKR for Boosting Career Success and Abundance: This symbol is one of prosperity, power, and protection. It only makes sense it is used to manifest abundance in all forms. There are testimonies of people who have manifested money using CKR. They had only to draw the symbol either on a piece of paper or on a currency note of high denomination. After this, they'd chant "Cho Ku Rei" three times, fold the note, draw another CKR symbol to seal the energy, and then place it in a special section of their wallet.

CKR can empower affirmations, business cards, meetings, clients, Facebook profiles, business logos, conference halls, and gadgets. This helps ward off the evil eye, prevent misfortune in business, and protect against psychic attacks.

CKR for Expressing Gratitude: Visualize every good thing and person that has come your way in life. Imagine them being suspended in white light or the sky through meditation. Set your intention for gratitude and seal it with the CKR symbol. You can amplify the effects of CKR by using serene meditation music for about 10 minutes.

Using CKR in Daily Life: I would suggest you try drawing CKR on your food and drinks. This is because consumables contain water, which is the only compound capable of existing in the three states of matter, and that goes against the earth's gravitational force. Water holds memories and energy. Thus, you want to be sure you are not polluting your physical form with negativity.

This cleansing should also take place even when you prepare the meals yourself. Besides the energy in the food or drink, you also imprint energy on consumables via touch and through the utensils used to make or serve the dish. Before consuming anything, invoke Reiki and place your hand above the food for 10 minutes to cleanse it and amp up its nutritional value. There is a possibility that doing this to drinks may slightly alter the taste from the original. But what's a little change in flavor compared to a psychically fortified dish?

CKR can reduce the side effects of medicines, reduce EMF on electronic devices, and encourage plant growth. Plants and meals are not the only things that can benefit from a Reiki pill. Even relationship problems can be fixed using Reiki. With CKR, you can strengthen the bonds in your relationships. One way of doing this is by drawing the symbol on pictures of your family members, friends, or loved ones. This helps build confidence, peace, acceptance, and trust.

CKR for Protection: Using CKR in your home protects you from burglary, theft, and negative thoughts. Draw it in the center of each room, on every wall, the top and bottom corners of each room, the ceilings, and the floors. You can take things a step further by engraving the symbol on the décor in the house or stitching it onto the drapes.

To amplify the symbol, you can use protective gemstones such as agate, apache tears, jet, rainbow moonstone, citrine quartz, obsidian, malachite, smoky quartz, black tourmaline, or hematite, among others. Draw CKR onto crystals to enhance their energy.

Alternate or Reverse Cho Ku Rei

Have you ever heard of optical isomerism in chemistry? This is a phenomenon where two or more compounds mirror one another yet perform different functions or possess different properties. That's what reverse CKR is, a mirrored version of the normal CKR.

Reverse CKR flushes out energy or light from an object, a place, or a living being. Reversing the spiral eliminates energy when it is present in surplus; hence alternate CKR is not advised for regular use or therapy except in special situations like a hyperactive patient. Here, using alternate CKR would induce fatigue or sleep.

Understand that there is no right or wrong way to draw the Cho Ku Rei if your intentions are clear. Suppose you visualize the alternate CKR during a session instead of the original one. There, it wouldn't matter, as the power of your intention will dictate the result of its application.

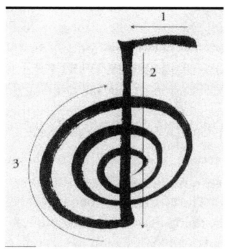

Reverse Cho-Ku-Rei

Chapter Three: The Mental-Emotional Symbol — Sei-He-Ki (SHK)

This is the second Reiki symbol. It represents emotional healing, purification, clarity, and protection from malignant forces. When translated, this symbol means "as above, so below," or "earth and sky coming together." Its spiritual meaning is "God and man become one," or "the key to the universe." The Sei-He-Ki symbol is regarded as the path to healing the subconscious.

Healing the consciousness is not done in conventional hospitals. It is an aspect of healing highly overlooked. Conjuring SHK channels Reiki to the emotions awakens the source within, changes your thought patterns, heightens your vibrational field, and heals the mind-body connection. This symbol is famous for ridding us of negativity, energy blocks, cravings, addictions, and other harmful behavioral patterns.

Drawing Sei-He-Ki

- Draw a three-part zig-zag line, as shown in strokes 1,2, and 3.

- Draw a vertical line from top to bottom, as in stroke 4. This line should meet the last zig-zag line from stroke 3.

- Draw a curved line from top to bottom. This line must join stroke 4 to become stroke 5.

- Draw another curved line from top to bottom. Refer to stroke 6. This line should be drawn a little distance from strokes 1 to 5. This 6th stroke should be parallel to others.

- Draw two curved lines like domes or half circles on stroke 6. If drawn correctly, the symbol should look something like this:

Sei-he-ki Symbol

SHK is used in conjunction with or immediately after the CKR symbol over a client's body to bring healing to their energy field's emotional and mental states. It balances their aura and their physical body. SHK can also be used after completing a healing session to bring harmony to an affected person's chakra, such as the heart chakra.

To heal this way, stand beside the Reiki treatment table and place a hand underneath your client's back at the level of his heart chakra. With your other hand, draw the CKR, then the SHK Reiki symbols a few inches above your patient's heart chakra. Listen carefully for their flow of energy. Please pay close attention to the moment their energy becomes steady before moving on to another position or chakra continuing your treatment.

Diving Deeper into Sei-He-Ki

Sei-He-Ki has its roots in Siddham, a Sanskrit word that means "perfected or accomplished." It is a medieval Brahmi script used by Japanese Shignon Buddhists to write down sutras and mantras. In Japan, the Siddham script is called bonji. On his spiritual journey, Usui Sensei became familiar with this and introduced the SHK symbol to heal the mind. SHK may have originated from the siddham script, but the Japanese use the pronunciation Sei-He-Ki and not the original Sanskrit pronunciation.

The kanji description of SHK translates to "correcting habits," pointing to the symbol's effectiveness in mental healing. Sei-He-Ki is a rather odd-looking symbol. Reiki historians claim that the Sei-He-Ki symbol design is based on the Japanese Buddhist goddess Kannon, the Bodhisattva of mercy and compassion who reaches out to beings in distress.

Practitioners say it resembles a bow and arrow that shoots directly into the heart. Some others liken it to the face and head of a man with the humps resembling two top knots of hair. Despite the metaphors, its use remains constant, establishing emotional and mental balance intended to communicate with our higher consciousness. This symbol serves two primary purposes:

> • It helps you or your client discover the emotions causing a physical, psychological, or emotional imbalance.

- It allows you to create balance by reorganizing your negative thought patterns, replacing them with positive habits and responses. When used with other symbols, SHK could cause energy shifts, as each sign possesses its unique vibrational frequency.

All physical illnesses have deep emotional roots that must be addressed for total well-being. Thoughts are pure energy, and emotions can be likened to energy constellations. When you are happy, you glow and radiate pure joy. When the reverse is the case, you grow dimmer, darker, gloomier. You are afraid to seek understanding or closure. You might even pretend to forget, doing such a great job you convince yourself that such an event never happened, or that all is well.

These painful feelings never go away. Like wounds, they fester and become smelly sores. They grow so out of proportion they manifest in the physical realm as a disease. Here's an example of how that happens. Steve has a nagging wife. When they were still in the dating phase, she would hound him for every petty reason under the sun. Still, Steve loved his girl, so he would keep mum and swallow her insults to keep the peace. He knew that if he uttered even a single syllable in self-defense, his house would become an arena, and his lady would assemble the calvary — her siblings and friends, who were always on her side.

After years of exclusive dating, Steve and his lady got married. Shortly after, instead of an extended honeymoon, he was diagnosed with advanced esophageal cancer. This is no coincidence.

You may have encountered many situations where lying on your bed at night or while in a safe space, you recall events of your day, getting angry for not standing up more for yourself, or responding to certain occurrences or people as you should have.

This "coulda-woulda-shoulda" mentality leads to a stockpile of guilt in your psyche. The bottled-up guilt leads to anxiety, then stress, depression, and later physical disease. Even scientists — the most nonhippie people you will ever meet — have managed to draw a connection between a host of physical afflictions and frustrations, loneliness, grief, and even fear. This is where SHK comes in. This symbol will help you when you feel distraught, upset, or emotionally out of sorts. It works by channeling divinity into your energy patterns, aligning your chakras in a way other signs fail to do. Unlike other Reiki symbols, SHK has fewer variations of its drawings. There is only one drawing that depicts it being slightly longer, but that's it.

Your pet can also manifest disease. Physical disease for them sometimes may be due to unreleased emotions or because of transference. This means that your pet is entirely capable of falling ill because you are sick or emotionally distraught. Pets have souls, too, and even though they can be trained to perform a few tricks, they have feelings and experience emotions like how humans do. They don't have the intellect or control to express them as we do.

However, if your pet is bonded to you, these negative emotions increase their frustration to the extent that they choose to sacrifice their bodies instead, taking upon their frail bodies the pain of your unresolved feelings and lingering negative energy. SHK can be used on both humans and animals to release emotional burdens so a prevailing physical illness ceases to manifest.

Using SHK to Heal Yourself Mentally

- Hold your hands out and place your palms on the very top of your head, the location of your crown chakra.

- Imagine the SHK and CKR symbols on your palms. Both must be used together as CKR is the switch that empowers and heightens the effects of SHK.

- Chant Cho-Ku-Rei thrice, then Sei-He-Ki thrice, now chant Cho-Ku-Rei thrice again.

- Continue the chant from the previous step for as long as you want the healing Reiki energy to flow. It is possible that while doing this, you may notice a slight vibrational change in the Reiki energy as it penetrates your soul. That is precisely the job of Reiki under the influence of SHK, targeting your mental and emotional issues. When this is done with pure intention for 15 to 20 minutes daily, all negative emotional entanglements are illuminated, becoming visible enough for you to make a well-informed choice: *To let go for the greater good.*

Using SHK on Others

After mastering the art of using SHK on yourself, you can now explore the option of practicing it on others. Do not force this on anyone or try to impose your belief in Reiki on another. Doing this would be only manipulation. You need to gently inform them this form of healing is available should they choose to try. If your gentle nudge aligns with their free will, they will accept your offer of mental healing when the time is right.

Before using SHK on another, ask if there is a particularly emotional issue they wish to resolve. If so, direct Reiki under the influence of SHK to fix it.

Remember, there is no need for exact details of their emotional problems since you are a holistic healer, not a therapist. It is not your job (no matter how loud your Nancy Drew meter pings) to listen or probe them for juicy tidbits. You only need to offer to heal. Considering your true intentions, Reiki will do the work all on its own. If your patient does not have a specific emotional intention by any chance, use the symbols CKR and SHK to channel Reiki for the client's general well-being.

In this, no matter how masterful a practitioner you are, never manipulate others with Reiki. The consequences of doing so are dire. You might even lose your gift. Another is that when you draw the SHK symbol between you and another, most of the other person's energy may rub off on you. This could have positive or negative effects depending on your intentions as a practitioner. Since you can't tell which way the proverbial pendulum will swing, you must do a cleansing ritual after each session.

Uses of Sei-He-Ki

It improves memory: Two SHK symbols drawn facing each other mimic both the left and right sides of the brain:

Double SHK Symbol

When SHK is used with CKR, SHK helps balance both brain hemispheres. SHK is believed to help make connections between both halves of the brain.

To improve memory, draw the symbols CKR, SHK, and another CKR on your third eye and give Reiki for about ten minutes each day. Stabilize the energy using a positive affirmation such as "my intuition, memory, and concentration increase by leaps and bounds each day."

It heals addictions and releases emotional blockages: Addictions such as nail-biting, smoking, excessive drinking, drug misuse, eating disorders, and gluttony are resolved using Sei-He-Ki. This is possible because SHK is the gateway to the subconscious. The power of this symbol helps you gradually understand and eventually come to love and accept yourself. Little wonder it is employed in weight loss. Since this symbol functions to amplify mental energy and emotional release, it would do you good to have a box of tissues handy during a session to prepare for the waterworks that might come.

To heal addictions, draw the CKR+SHK+CKR symbol on the heart chakra and channel Reiki for 15 minutes daily. Stabilize this energy with a positive affirmation such as "I am healed of my addictions and release of all negative behaviors, surrendering them to the divine for my greatest good."

It clears negative energy and rids you of karmic attachments: A space, pet, or a person can have residual spiritual attachments or discarnate entities. These attachments could be karmic. The entities are commonly called ghosts.

Whether you agree there is such a thing as ghosts or not, some entities are stuck in our dimension, lingering because of some unresolved issue or tasks left on earth after their passing, keeping them from moving on. Some of these entities can be mischievous or downright harmful when left to their devices. They cause havoc because of their advantage of being invisible to the spiritually unaware.

Karmic attachments, on the other hand, can be negative energy situations or diseases accumulated from previous lifetimes. Without dissolving these attachments, you cannot have a truly fulfilling relationship with your present. Using the SHK symbol can help dispel these negative entities, bonds, or energies, healing you without your being aware of it. You can draw the CKR in conjunction with the SHK on yourself and in all corners of your space to protect against psychic manipulation.

It improves relationships: Because this symbol resonates with the emotions, it improves communication in relationships, calms arguments, and removes feelings of sadness, nervousness, anger, and fear.

Its vibration — slightly higher than CKR — makes SHK a powerful symbol for creating harmony, opening dimensions, and healing on all levels. Raising your vibration using this symbol can fight feelings of depression by acting as a barrier against all the negativity that provides the prime environment for despondency.

Transferring Sei-He-Ki from Yourself to Another

- Visualize a luminescent SHK symbol radiating from your Ajna chakra to the back of your palms before assuming different hand positions and resting them on your patient.

- Imagine a bright light illuminating the SHK symbol all around. Imagine its reflection on your hands before starting a hands-on session with your patient.

- Draw the symbol using your tongue on the roof of your mouth, then project said symbol onto your palms as they rest on your client's form

- Draw the SHK symbol in the air using your index finger, leading Reiki in the direction of your choosing.

- Draw the symbol onto the palms of your hands using your index finger before placing it on your client.

The caveat for transferring the SHK symbol is like the one given when transferring CKR. Only a Reiki practitioner or second-degree Reiki initiate should see you drawing these symbols, no one else. Activating the sign is a necessary step taken to ensure its efficacy.

To activate SHK, you must begin by drawing the light switch, CKR. Chant CKR silently three times, after which you should outline the SHK symbol as you silently chant it thrice as well. After this, seal the energy with another CKR symbol, silently chanting Cho-Ku-Rei thrice as you do so.

Chapter Four: The Connecting or Distant Healing Symbol — Hon-Sha-Ze-Sho-Nen

The correct way to pronounce the third Reiki symbol known as Hon Sha Ze Sho Nen is "*Han Sha Zei Sho Nen.*" This symbol has many calligraphic variations, all depending on the brush style of the person drawing it. As a result, it is the most complicated second-degree Reiki symbol, and students need a bit of time to master and understand it.

It comprises five different Chinese characters. Japan had no script of its own during the introduction of Buddhism in the sixth century. For this reason, Japan adopted the Chinese calligraphy, applying it to their language, calling it kanji.

Each character in this symbol is unique enough to create its complex meaning. Loosely put, it means "the divinity in me salutes the divinity in you" or "there is no past, present or future," establishing the connection between our true selves devoid of ego that transcends all time and space. Each kanji incorporated in HSZSN represents the five elements and the chakras of the human body.

Drawing the Hon-Sha-Ze-Sho-Nen Symbol

Let's analyze all three parts of this structure.

For the Kanji Symbols, HON:

1. Draw a straight two-inch line from top to bottom. This stroke signifies the beginning. Eternity begins here.

2. From right to left, draw a straight three-inch line across the stroke. This second stroke in Japanese kanji signifies ten, meaning "the end" or "completion," as the Japanese only count till ten.

3. In the left lower quadrant, draw another one-inch line angled at 45 degrees. The line should be drawn from right to left and from up to down.

4. Do the same on the right lower quadrant. When combined with the first and second, the third and fourth strokes denote a tree, which represents the tree of life and timelessness.

5. Draw a half-inch long horizontal line from left to right. This line should cross the bottom part of the stroke. This last stroke signifies the root of the tree, its very essence or origin. When drawn correctly, it should resemble this:

For the Kanji Symbol, SHA:

1. Draw a three-inch-long horizontal line from left to right directly below stroke five to form six.

2. Draw another three-inch-long line cutting swiftly on the far right of stroke six. This line should curve gently downwards, swinging till it terminates at the left side of six, directly beneath it by half an inch (7).

3. In the middle section of the page, draw a straight line two-and-a-half inches long directly below stroke seven, from left to right (8).

4. On the left side of stroke eight, draw a three-inch-long straight line from top to bottom. This line must meet stroke eight at its top (9).

5. On the right side of stroke eight, draw another three-inch-long straight line from top to bottom. This line must meet stroke eight at its top (10).

6. Halfway up the right side of stroke ten, from left to right, draw a straight half-inch line (11).

7. Slightly below this "tent," from left to right, draw an inch-long line starting from the left of stroke ten. This makes stroke 12. When correctly drawn, it will resemble this:

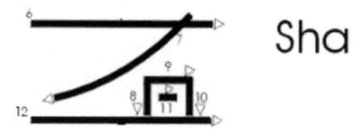

The Kanji Symbols ZE, SHO, And NEN

This segment of the Reiki symbol resembles a house with a smiley face on the inside.

1. On the right side of stroke 12, directly beneath but not quite touching stroke 9, draw a straight one-inch-long straight line from top to bottom (13).

2. Halfway upstroke 13, at the right of the line, draw a straight line, a quarter of an inch long from left to right (14).

3. On the left side of those, directly below but not quite touching stroke 12, draw a line a quarter of an inch long from top to bottom (15).

4. In the middle of the page, draw a three or four-inch-long line from top to bottom. This line should curve gently from left to right. The resulting stroke will form the right side of the house (16).

5. On the left side, half an inch away from the tip of the stroke 16, from top to bottom, draw another line that gently curves from left to right (17). This stroke completes the house.

6. Inside the tent on the left side, three-quarters of an inch from the top, draw a quarter-inch long line from left to right (18).

7. This next stroke will resemble a big number seven, except that the top of the seven and its long part will be gently curved. On the left side of the house, half an inch away from and below stroke 18, draw the tip of the seven close to the house's wall. Bring the curved end of the seven inwards a quarter of an inch from left to right.

8. From top to bottom, gently curve the long part of the seven from left to right following the line of the house (12 to 19).

---

9. On the lower right side inside the house, draw a half-inch long line from right to left curved like the smile on a happy face emoji (20).

10. On the left side above stroke 21, draw a quarter-inch long line from top to bottom. This line should curve slightly inwards from right to left (21).

11. On the right side and above stroke 21, draw a quarter-inch long line from top to bottom. This line should curve slightly inwards from left to right (22).

12. Strokes 21 and 22 will be the lines that form the eyes on the happy face. These curves will face each other. This completes the Ze-Sho-Nen. Appropriately drawn, it would resemble this:

When the entire symbol is put together, you have Hon-Sha-Ze-Sho-Nen

Hon

Sha

Ze

Sho

Nen

Diving Deeper Into HON-SHO-ZE-SHO-NEN (HSZSN)

The HSZSN symbol resembles a tall pyramid known in East-Asia as a pagoda or a stupa, a dome-shaped Buddhist structure used as a place of meditation and for the storage of sacred relics. Many Reiki historians claim that the symbol translates to a sentence that means "no past, no present, no future."

Even physicists believe that if time could be charted on a graph in the form of a curve, extending this curve long enough will bring the past to meet up with the future. Let's break this symbol down literally.

- Hon: book, truth, real, origin, to find the essence of

- Sha: someone, person, who, which, he/she who is

- Ze: correct, justice, right, perfect, just so

- Sho: Righteous, straight, basis of real knowledge

- Nen: Feelings, thoughts, memory, meditative wisdom, forbearance or patience

It's about pondering our very essence, so we can take back the wisdom originally ours, to begin with. The kanji Hon corresponds with the element of wood. The kanji Sha matches fire, Ze matches

Earth, Sho is represented by metal, and Nen by water. The power in the five elements is encompassed within this Reiki symbol. Each element has close associations with the phenomenon of life both in the theoretical and practical sense.

This symbol acts as an emblem that guides us to our true selves. It is proof that focusing on our most authentic selves exposes us to the genuine wisdom inherent in us. All that is needed is the activation of this knowledge. This symbol teaches that deep within, we are already whole and aware and aren't lacking knowledge. New things can be learned from books, fellow seekers, and other sources of knowledge, but do this for the pure joy of the experience and nothing else.

Many Reiki practitioners believe that HSZSN only works for distance healing, but that is only one use of this potent symbol. This third symbol contains spiritual energy, which transmits Reiki energy regardless of space, time, and distance.

Like the SHK symbol, the HSZSN must be activated using CKR. This way, the practitioner is granted the ability to channel Reiki energy to a client seated before them or far away in another continent. During distance healing, all three symbols must be used. Activate Reiki with CKR, create harmony and balance with SHK, channel Reiki to bridge the distance between space, dimensions, and time using HSZSN.

When conducting distance healing for a person, if the person is open-minded enough, they are likely to feel the effects of Reiki energy. Distance healing does not take as long as hands-on healing sessions, but this does not imply they are less effective. It is possible to set a time limit for distance healing sessions, empower and renew them daily.

Uses of HON-SHA-ZE-SHO-NEN

Help Heal Past Wounds: Distance is no barrier to Reiki as we have already established. It is possible to send energy to the past to heal traumatic events. You must understand that Reiki energy is not a time machine. It will not go back in time and, like an eraser, ensure those hurtful events never occurred. Instead, under the influence of HSZSN, it will help you reassess those situations and help you see things from a new perspective. This way, you heal your hurt and let go of your pain.

Help Prepare for Future Circumstances: You can use this symbol to prepare for situations that have not happened yet. Like a battery, Reiki stores energy to access them later. Are you scared of dental appointments? Send Reiki ahead of you to calm you ahead of your doctor's appointment. You can use this method for job interviews, examinations, and meetings with business associates. It helps you stay on the sunny side of things despite your fear.

Help with Distant Healing: This is also called absentee healing. Reiki can heal a person or people not in the same room as you. Distance healing is of great use when a patient is quarantined for health reasons, such as a highly infectious disease or third-degree burns.

People may also want a high degree of privacy and may not take kindly to a one-on-one physical session. Distance healing has proven helpful for calming wild animals and even pets who do not wish to be touched. These are both situations where either you or the client can develop a secondary infection or injury via physical contact.

Your patient could be in a different country or continent and receive the effects of Reiki energy. You can also heal the earth, sending this divine energy to heal victims of accidents, terrorist attacks, or war. Here, your intention should be a peaceful conflict resolution for all parties involved. You can also send Reiki to the families of all affected by these occurrences visualizing them being pain free so they cope better and heal from the effects of war.

Heal the Earth: You can send Reiki to mother earth to heal the world from the dangers of deforestation, poaching, forest fires, oil spillage, and illegal sea or land mining. It goes a long way in healing the delicate ecosystem from these human-made disasters. Sending Reiki in these instances is your way of giving love back to mother nature that has given you so much yet asked nothing in return.

Support Those Who Have Passed Away: Channeling the same sequence of Reiki symbols to send light towards the greater good of family friends or clients who have died enables us to help them wherever they are. Reiki helps them heal and evolve even though they are on a higher spiritual plane compared to us. All you need is 10 to 15 minutes of Reiki distance healing. This may seem little at first, but it helps a lot.

Channeling Reiki is not meant for communication but as a way of sending healing and spiritual support. The beauty of Reiki is its flexibility. Practitioners use distant healing in a myriad of ways. It would be best if you found a way that works for you.

Gain Access to Akashic Records: The Akashic records are also called the Book of God's Remembrance or the Book of Life. These records contain an account of thoughts, events, words, intent, and emotions that have happened, present, and future. The Akashic records also contain the karmic attachments, goals, contracts, and debts of every human. A series of healing sessions using the third symbol of Reiki can uncover and release karmic agreements and resolve karmic debts.

I would strongly recommend not accessing these records as a new initiate or a beginner. Information contained in these records is enormous and outstanding, like data on a supercomputer. These records are the universe's supercomputer. There is a wealth of information available in these records, both good and bad. For this reason, only third-degree Reiki users or master level Reiki practitioners should be allowed this form of access.

To access these records, cleanse yourself and activate a layer of protection on all your energy centers. Use the sequence of Reiki symbols CKR+SHK+HSZSN and do deep breathing exercises to calm your mind and allow you to enter the alpha state. Only in this state can the conscious mind be quietened enough to receive messages from the spiritual realm. If you access these records helped by spirit guides, remember to thank your guides for their support.

Using the Third Symbol on Yourself

You can use the distant healing symbol in your life in so many ways:

Send Reiki to Your Past: Use the HSZSN symbol to send Reiki back to your past, situations, or events where you experienced trauma or suffering, such as the death of a loved one, or a failure in your life. Sending Reiki to those periods in your past soothe you, bringing relief and removing any form of blockage affecting your present. This healing process can be liberating as it helps you exorcise your past, inner demons.

There are two ways of sending Reiki healing energy to our past.

• Take a trip back to the traumatic event and imagine yourself as a spectator. Intone the CKR+SHK+HSZSN symbols intending to heal and rid you of all negative psychological imprints left by past events. Visualize joy and happiness for 5 to 10 minutes as you are brought from the darkness into the light.

• On a piece of paper, write down a short description of the traumatic event. Fold the paper neatly into a square that fits right in the palm of your hands. Apply the sequence of Reiki symbols and visualize directing the healing energy to the event and any present problems resulting from your experience. Dissolve the negative energies for your greater good and the good of others involved.

When sending Reiki into the past, I strongly advise that it does not become a daily practice. You aim to purify yourself from the bonds of your history and not change or deny them. Do this process for ten minutes, twice a week, tops. Regularly sending a large amount of Reiki to past events will expose you to the risk of bringing back aspects of the past into your present.

Reiki in Your Present: Sometimes in life, you could suffer lethargy and be in dire need of an energy boost. In this situation, you need to take time off to meditate for a few minutes. In those minutes, you can send Reiki energy by visualizing the white light of Reiki energy enveloping and healing your entire body, every cell, tissue, muscle, and organ from your crown chakra to your feet.

Draw the CKR and HSZSN on your energy centers to invite Reiki to heal, cleanse, and intensely purify, filling you with energy. The crown chakra is the gateway to all the other chakras. Using the symbols on the top of your forehead opens a spiritual path towards your highest self.

Reiki for Your Future: It is possible to send energy to your future self. You can go days, weeks, months, or years into your future and prepare ahead for the occurrences. Look at your social, personal, or business calendar and pick an event. This event can be your retirement, a vacation, or a wedding. Even if you have no specific date or event in mind, you can send Reiki to attract favor, success, and fortune in your future.

Often, when you send Reiki to yourself in the past, present, or future, you receive a message, validation, or acknowledgment. This "sign" may become as clear as a voice in your head, presenting a successful conclusion to your reason for sending Reiki. This sign will help ease your worries, bringing about a feeling of calm and confidence. Practice using HSZSN or any Reiki symbol on yourself first to gain the benefits before trying it on anyone else.

Conducting a Distance Healing Session

Before performing a distance healing session, it is essential to obtain permission from the individual you intend to heal. Never channel Reiki to an unwilling person. Only after securing consent can you search for a quiet environment, free of all disturbances. Decide on the form of distant healing you want to use before sending Reiki energy. Only then can you begin the session. Some ways of conducting distance healing are:

- Hold an object that belongs to the target person in your hands to connect to her and send distance healing. You can use a doll for this or something similar. Whether animate or inanimate objects are used, all items possess consciousness.

- Use yourself as a surrogate. Place your hands over your body to heal your client. Move your hands filled with Reiki to each area of the body you feel your patient needs healing, like in a real session.

- Use a photo of your client. Activate the Reiki in your palms and open the gateway of universal life force between you and your client. Let the photo rest for 15 minutes in your cupped palms or for as long as a session lasts.

- Create an image of your client in your mind's eye. After activating Reiki, open the gateway using the three symbols CKR+ SHK+ HSZSN for 15 to 20 minutes or for as long as a session lasts.

- If, by any chance, you draw the HSZSN wrong or any other Reiki symbol do not cancel the session or start over. Reiki energy is intelligent, and the issue will be fixed as honest efforts and intentions are needed, not exact replications, but this is not an excuse to disrespect the symbols or be lazy about memorizing them. There is a reason the signs are sacred. They are writings representing very ancient energy.

When conducting a distance healing session, remember to ground yourself and connect with the universal life force. You would need to connect with this energy, both spiritually and mentally. For this to happen, you need to leave your ego behind and remember you are simply a conduit for the power.

Remember to feel the flow of Reiki before you proceed with the healing session. Keep the session in place for as long as you think it should continue. The average time for this is about 15 to 20 minutes. Always make sure the session is conducted not for your ego but the patient's greatest good. HSZSN works with the conscious mind and the mental body, unlike SHK that works with the subconscious mind. Before using the HSZSN, it is essential you or your patient understands the full picture and has resolved their hidden emotional dilemma; only after this can HSZSN offer you or the other person new directions, actions, and choices.

This is because, to change the present and possibly the future, you must first deal with the past. Like the typical domino effect, once you resolve the past, the present and future also fall in line. When using this symbol, understand that esoterically, there is no past, present, or future; all time is here and now.

End the distance healing session by positively visualizing the healing of the person, space, or situation you focused on. After completing the session, hand over the outcomes to infinite love, wisdom, or the spirit of Reiki. Disconnect from the session by washing your hands in cold running water or flapping your hands vigorously to cut off the Reiki energy. Drink water to stay hydrated and connect yourself to the earth.

Channeling Reiki

As you practice Reiki and your practice becomes busier with more clients coming in for treatments, requests, or workshops, you will receive more calls for distant Reiki. You will need to become more creative in finding ways to handle the extra workload.

You must seek ways to juggle the traditional healing of multiple clients, events, or situations. For instance, you may have requested from people in other countries for Reiki. These clients may request healing either for the present or future occasions such as weddings, and child dedications. It would be time-consuming to provide healing to them all at separate times due to time zone differences. To do this, you will need to combine their requests and send them simultaneously. Think of this as sending a bulk SMS. This saves you a lot of time and effort. Some creative ways distance healing can be conducted for multiple individuals include:

Using a Reiki Box: Pen down the clients' names or the situations you intend to send healing. Include the dates and times of Reiki requests and put the paper containing their names into a box with the clients photographs if you can get them. You can ask that they send along a photo with their request via email.

Channel Reiki to this box regularly. This way, Reiki is sent to all the recipients in the box. If you don't have a box, you can use a porcelain pot with a lid or any other container if it is solely designated for Reiki. Keep the box in a safe space, and if you can, surround it with healing crystals and set aside time each day to send healing to those clients.

Check the box and read through the cards regularly because some clients need the Reiki boost for a short period while others will need it for the rest of their lives. Use your intuition to pick through each card and stop Reiki once the clients inform you of progress. Add your aspirations or that of your close family and friends experiencing illness or other challenges in life.

Using a Reiki Board: Are you familiar with vision boards? With vision boards, you can see your dreams and aspirations briefly and manifest them using the law of attraction. You can apply the same principle by making a collage of the names and photographs of people you wish to heal.

Use thumbtacks, glue, or tape to attach their names and photos. After which, you can "beam" Reiki to them from the comfort of your home or office. You can charge your Reiki board with crystals reinforced with energy, place the charged crystals in a set pattern around the Reiki board, and intone specific intentions before sending healing.

Always try to share your distant healing experiences with past or future clients if appropriate. Prospective clients could benefit from any information or insights you may have experienced during distant Reiki healing. It is also possible to benefit from feedback, be it positive or negative. Positive feedback reminds you that you are doing something right. Negative feedback helps you fine-tune your technique to benefit your clients.

The Reiki Sandwich

Wouldn't it be superb if psychic energy found our way into the menu at our favorite coffee shop or restaurant? Don't you wish that all you had to do was place an order for some Reiki to-go when you felt tired? While you debate whether a Reiki sandwich would taste better than a Reiki salad, I must burst your bubble. This "energy boost" may be called a sandwich, but it's far from edible.

The method you employ in using any of the Reiki symbols depends heavily on your Reiki lineage. Your lineage is the system or line of teaching your teacher was trained in. In certain lineages, you are instructed to use all three symbols regardless of the hand positions you adopt during a healing session. Some other masters opine that the second symbol should be employed only in exceptional circumstances.

The Reiki sandwich is an arrangement or a Reiki energy healing technique where the symbols are piled one on top of the other or used in combination to boost the effectiveness of a single symbol. This is possible because each symbol possesses a specific vibration that is a recipe for harnessing pure power when put together.

Drawing a Reiki Sandwich

- Activate Reiki by drawing the Cho Ku Rei

- Draw the second symbol you desire beside or beneath the first symbol

- Seal the energy with another Cho Ku Rei beside or beneath the second symbol. There you have it! Your psychic sandwich to-go.

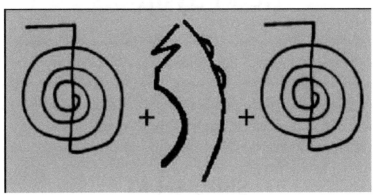

A Reiki Sandwich

Using A Reiki Sandwich

Intone each symbol three times and imagine Reiki energy beaming from your Ajna chakra into the Ajna chakra of your patient. As you silently intone each sign, add intentions only for your patient's mind and body's highest good.

Reiki sandwiches are used for a host of reasons, the most popular being the healing of addictions, weight loss, gaining clarity, or seeking solutions to problematic issues and releasing mental and emotional blocks in your patient before the holistic healing begins.

Chapter Five: Non-Traditional Reiki Symbols

Non-traditional Reiki symbols are those discovered by practitioners not under the umbrella of Usui Shiki Ryoho. They are not part of the characters taught and passed down through Mrs. Hawayo Takata. These symbols are taught in other schools of Reiki. Shika-Sei-Ki and Shika-So are two essential symbols for opening and cleansing the heart, soul, communication, and fostering emotional connections.

Shika-Sei-Ki

Shika-Sei-Ki serves the role of purifying your heart and soul. It is fondly called the Reiki symbol for peace. This symbol resonates with the heart chakra, also known as Anahata or the fourth chakra. It can concentrate considerable energy.

Shika-Sei-Ki has physical and spiritual functions. Physically, it helps heal cardiovascular ailments such as myocardial or pericardial inflammations, ischemic heart disease, and abnormal heart rhythms. Spiritually, it increases your ability to give and receive love by flooding your heart chakra with divine light. It also provides you with a sense of calm and inner tranquility.

Shika-Sei-Ki connects us with all aspects of our soul, especially in anxiety, stress, depression, anger, and mistrust. This is the symbol employed when we grieve over the passing of a loved one, a terrible breakup, or when we feel nostalgia over having to leave a place in which we have become familiar. Activating Shika-Sei-Ki using Cho-Ku-Rei on your palms helps release all your feelings of vulnerability and opens your heart to the light of healing.

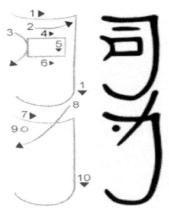

Drawing of Shika-Sei-Ki

Using Shika-Sei-Ki

Remember that sandwich we talked about? We can make another with Shika-Sei-Ki. We need only to tweak the "recipe."

- Switch on Reiki by drawing Cho-Ku-Rei. This will heighten the powers of the next symbol.

- Draw the Sei-He-Ki symbol to open the spiritual dimension and get rid of negative vibrations to create harmony

- Draw another Cho-Ku-Rei to seal Sei-He-Ki and activate the next symbol.

- Draw the Shika-Sei-Ki symbol to heal at the emotional level.

- Seal Shika-Sei-Ki using another Cho-Ku-Rei symbol and keep your hands on your patient for about 15 minutes.

Use Shika-Sei-Ki in homes to create a warm, peaceful environment. In relationships, placing an activated symbol of Shika-Sei-Ki on your lover's heart chakra and yours will foster harmony, better communication, and healing.

Shika-So

Shika-So resonates with the throat chakra, also known as the fifth chakra or Vishuddha, which is the energy center known for communication, honesty, and self-expression. Because of this, Shika-So is the symbol to connect with in communication, misunderstandings, and anxiety. It works with Shika-Sei-Ki to create spiritual balance.

Like Shika-Sei-Ki, Shika-So also has physical and spiritual benefits. Physically, this symbol helps in relieving ailments of the throat and thyroid such as sore throat, swollen lymph nodes, hypothyroidism and hyperthyroidism, neck pains, cough, and tonsillitis. Spiritually, it opens a conduit to effective communication. With this symbol, you learn to express yourself better, avoid the lone wolf syndrome (unless you are one by choice), increase your confidence, reduce and, in time, eliminate certain speech deficiencies such as stuttering.

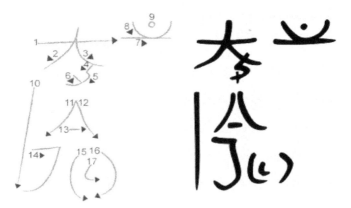

Drawing of Shika-So

Uses of Shika-So

- Drawing this symbol on your throat, chakra helps you stay mindful of the words you speak. Tact is not a gift everyone is born with. This symbol helps you know how to read a room and know when to talk, and when silence is the best option.

- When used with Cho-Ku-Rei, this symbol helps you express your thoughts in the best way. This helps curb misunderstandings.

- Shika-So, when used with Shika-Sei-Ki, helps you tap into your creative side. The reason is that both the heart and the throat chakra are connected in many ways. Passion and creativity are unleashed with these two signs.

- Drawing a sandwich of Cho Ku Rei, Shika-Sei-Ki, and Shika-So in a room helps the room occupants communicate and understand each other better. This is ideal for resolving family conflicts or avoiding tedious business meetings.

Nin-Giz-Zida

A Reiki Symbol with Many Names: The Serpent of Fire, Mae Loong, the Tibetan fire serpent, or fire dragon. This symbol is used in Tibetan, Karuna, and traditional Reiki in the attunement process, but its use varies according to Reiki lineage.

Generally, every attunement process begins with the Tibetan fire serpent. This symbol is drawn on the crown chakra and the back chakra. Its purpose is simply to awaken your Kundalini, which is divine feminine energy coiled at the base of the spine, or Muladhara that awakens you to the divine truth and infinite wisdom dwelling within you.

Kundalini can be awoken with Yoga and other spiritual practices such as Reiki. This awakening allows Reiki to flow seamlessly in all chakras simultaneously. The connection to Kundalini is why the

Tibetan fire serpent is used to open the recipient's chakras during the attunement. Other symbols could open the energy channels, but only this symbol opens them all at once. This symbol is used in the clearing of energy centers towards the recipient's crown chakra, allowing harmony and alignment between all energy centers, leaving you feeling cleansed and energized at the spiritual level.

The fire of Kundalini achieved using the Tibetan fire serpent helps you offer relief to humans and animals. This symbol is also useful in curbing symptoms of menopause, such as hot flushes, night sweats, and insomnia. Use the fire serpent to ease spinal problems and low back pain. You need only to activate the symbol and draw it over the spinal column, then channel Reiki for at least 15 minutes.

Drawing Nin-Giz-Zida

- Draw a straight two-inch-long line from left to right (1).

- To this, draw a connecting line that descends in a series of waves (2).

- At the base of stroke 2, draw a connecting line that terminates in two and a half anticlockwise spirals (3).

Drawing of Nin-Giz-Zida

Working consistently with this symbol brings a lot of changes. Since the energy centers align with each other, you will live a happy and carefree life.

Zonar

This symbol is pronounced Zoe-nar. It is the symbol of eternity or infinity. Zonar is the "lidocaine" of the spiritual realm, an anesthetic that heals emotional wounds resulting from the past, present, or future. Draw the symbol on the solar plexus chakra (stomach area) and the Manipura chakra (beneath the navel). It is also the symbol used to resolve karmic debts and inter-dimensional issues that defy explanation.

Drawing Zonar

This symbol resembles a letter Z. The last stroke of the Z rises to form the infinity symbol three times across the middle of the Z.

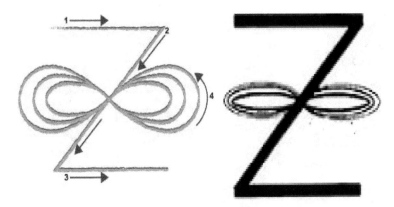

Drawing of Zonar

Uses of Zonar

- Its strong connection to the archangel Gabriel, the divine messenger, helps send energy during Reiki distance healing to dissolve karmic debts from the past that interfere in your current relationship.

- When drawn on the walls and ceilings of space, it has a spiritual shielding effect.

- Zonar is also used to heal diseases on a cellular level and resolve issues relating to child abuse.

Harth

This symbol rhymes with the word "Heart," and for a good reason. Harth is the Reiki symbol of compassion, infinite love, beauty, truth, and harmony. It is shaped like an anchor or a cross in a pyramid. It was first channeled by Marcy Miller and Kathleen Milner and is the primary symbol of Karuna-Ki Reiki. All its strokes are drawn from left to right and from top to bottom. You can use this symbol on the crown, Ajna, and heart chakra to open the highest, purest forms of divine love, energy, and vibration.

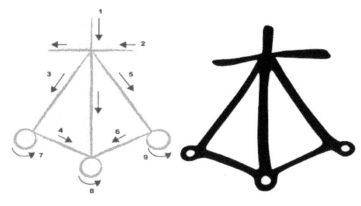

Drawing of Harth

Uses of Harth

- When drawn on the crown chakra, it rekindles your intuition and zest for life.

- It improves relationships by increasing your feelings of love and compassion towards others when drawn on the heart and throat chakras. It also fills you with positivity and diminishes cardiac problems.

- It helps heal addictions of all kinds by opening your heart and mind from the self-sabotaging behaviors and excuses you use to insulate yourself from the truth.

Halu

This symbol is pronounced hay-loo and is an amplified Zonar. This symbol means love, beauty, and truth. It is the symbol to use when breaking behavioral patterns to initiate deep causal, physical, and karmic healing.

Drawing Halu

Like the Zonar, it begins with a letter Z embedded with an infinity sign. Besides this, it has a pyramid at the top.

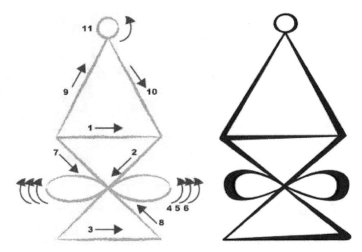

Drawing of Halu

Uses of Halu

- It helps you acknowledge your mistakes and take responsibility for your actions.

- Its close association with the archangel Raphael makes it a symbol for global and psychic protection.

- It allows us to recognize and change things not in line with our spiritual evolution.

- It offers protection against manipulative techniques and mental and physical stress.

Gnosa

This symbol is pronounced Know-Sa and is affiliated with angels of divine wisdom. The word Gnosa means spiritual and mystical knowledge gained through feeling and divine prophecy. Gnosa was revealed to Marie Abraham in a period of deep meditation. It increases intuition and clear the path to understanding when used on the Ajna and crown chakras.

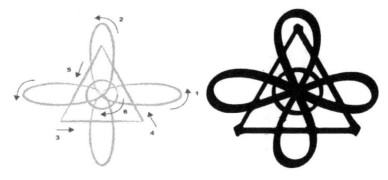

Drawing of Gnosa

Uses of Gnosa

- Drawing a double Gnosa on your crown chakra helps you recover from fatigue, relieves tension, helps you study and memorize better.

- It's time to ditch the hair of the dog! Drawing a Reiki sandwich containing Gnosa is useful in helping with hangovers.

- Gnosa helps you love and accept yourself in a non-narcissistic way.

Rama

This is the Reiki symbol for grounding or balance. The word Rama is coined from the Hindu word ram, which means God. Rama is affiliated with archangel Michael. It means abiding joy. It represents your tether to earth energy and the goddess Gaia. This symbol functions to purify living areas, eliminate energy blockages, clear out your lower six chakras, revive your life force or chi, and clear out negative energies.

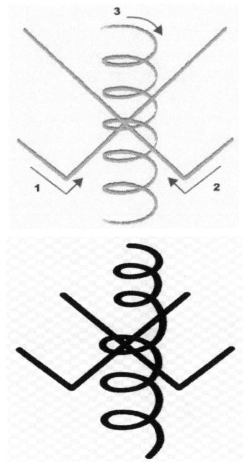

Drawing of Rama

Kriya

Pronounced Kree-Yah, this symbol means action and perfect balance. It comprises two Cho-Ku-Rei symbols facing one another. It is the Reiki for manifestation on the physical plane and the transformation of thoughts into reality.

It is said to share an affiliation with the angels of creativity. Kathleen Milner and William Rand first channeled it. When drawn on the crown chakra, it eliminates internal struggle, increasing your will to focus and transform your idea into action. When used with Hon-Sha-Ze-Sho-Nen, it is used in healing humans and the planet.

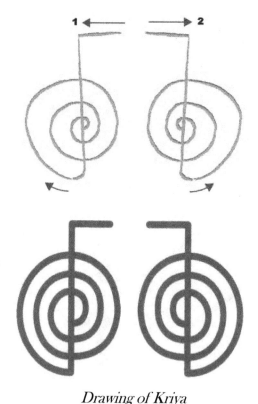

Drawing of Kriya

Lava

Pronounced Ee-Ah-Vah, this symbol rids one veil of illusions, lies, and conditioning. The four elements, earth, wind, water, fire, and spirit, are represented in this beautiful Reiki symbol, indicating harmony and interconnectedness. Lava activates the inner fire within you, helps you resist peer pressure, superstitious beliefs, and other negative influences, connecting you with your most authentic self.

Drawing of Lava

Aum (Or Om)

Pronounced Ah-uu-mm, this is more than a Sanskrit symbol used in various spiritual practices. Om is the master symbol for Karuna Reiki. It represents universal unity and a connection to divinity. It is regarded as the universe's sacred sound embodying all stages of physical manifestation: creation, preservation, and destruction.

Om serves many purposes, including self-mastery, healing, meditation, protection, psychic attunement for focused thought, purifying, and sealing the aura. When drawn on the crown chakra, it initiates you into the realm of higher consciousness. When used during Reiki attunement, it opens your primary energy channel (Sushumna) and crown chakra. Om is one of the most powerful mantras in existence.

Drawing of Aum

Shanti

Pronounced shahn-tee, this is a high vibrational symbol representing peace. Used on the third to seventh chakras and their projections, this symbol is associated with the angels of peace, harmony, and spiritual support. When used in tandem with Sei-He-Ki and Shika-Sei-Ki, they create balance in the environment. Shanti also helps with self-esteem problems, manifestation, insomnia, fear, and panic attacks.

Drawing of Shanti

Shamballa Reiki: Symbols for Multi-Dimensional Healing

This is another branch of Reiki with several non-traditional symbols. The term Shamballa describes a mythical realm either within our planet or in another dimension. This is a very high vibrational branch of Usui Reiki channeled by the count of Saint Germain, a European alchemist to John Armitage (also called by Hari Das Melchizedek or Hari Das Baba).

Shamballa Reiki has 352 known metaphysical levels derived from the lost city of Atlantis, each with its symbol revealed to only the most devoted of practitioners. This branch of Reiki has more mediations compared to Karuna Reiki. The signs offered devoted practitioners the highest energies ever known to humanity.

Shamballa Reiki Symbols

Mer Ka Fa Ka Lish Ma

This symbol is the manifestation of the divine mother or earth goddess. It has the power to realign and initiate healing on a genetic and chromosomal level. When used on the crown chakra, it grounds and connects you to Reiki. When drawn on the spinal column, it energizes all the chakras at once.

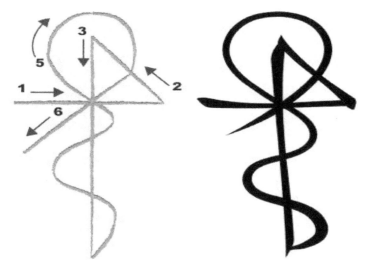

Drawing of Mer Ka Fa Ka Lish Ma

Motor Zanon

This is fondly called the anti-viral symbol. The word "motor" means entry, and "Zanon" means exit. I call this spiritual "penicillin." I don't mean penicillin is a cure-all, but I am sure you get my drift. When used with Cho-Ku-Rei, this unique sign can destroy bacteria, fungi, viruses, and several microorganisms.

This symbol is commonly used with Halu in providing relief from the symptoms of infectious diseases. To cure viral infections, draw a

Reiki sandwich as follows; Cho-Ku-Rei + Motor Zanon + reverse Cho-Ku-Rei. This way, polarity is reversed, and this symbol drags the bacteria or virus along with it. Some practitioners praise its effectiveness in exorcisms.

Drawing of Motor Zanon

Amsui

Amsui is the Shamballa symbol for completion. Credited to Bas Van Woelderen, this symbol is used where you need to adapt to new energies and vibrations in your journey to spiritual awakening.

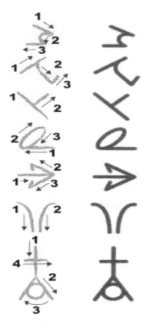

Drawing of Amsui

Ho Ka O Ili

This is the Shamballa Reiki symbol for self-respect, regality, and esteem.

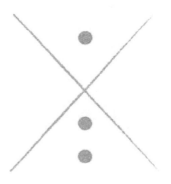

Ho Ka O Ili Symbol

Abundance

This is one of the most sought-after symbols, but use it lightly. Some people call this symbol the Midas star. The abundance symbol is one for self-growth, chasing away poverty, manifesting money, and spiritual wealth.

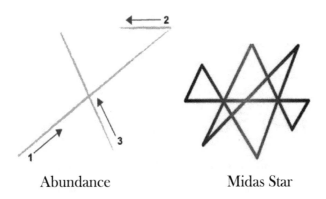

Abundance   Midas Star

Chapter Six: Byosen Scanning

Reiki may be a holistic healing method, its energy infinite, powerful, and all-knowing. But it is wrong and unethical to channel Reiki without permission from your client and without conducting an "energy sweep" to determine precisely where Reiki is needed.

One of the essential caveats in Reiki healing is that your ego should be left behind. In channeling energy, you are not a person but a channel, and all intentions are done for the highest good. Sending Reiki without permission or doing a Byosen is tantamount to spiritual "assault." Byosen Reikan Ho is a Japanese Reiki practice typically taught in second-degree Reiki or Okuden. Byosen Reikan ho comprises of five Japanese Kanji, namely:

- Byo — sickness, disease

- Sen — present, uniform

- Rei — spirit, sacred

- Kan — impressions, sensations

- Ho — system, method, rule

Putting together all the Kanji, Byosen Reikan-Ho would mean "sickness present spirit impressions system." This is quite a mouthful that's a bit too disjointed to allow for proper comprehension. A better way of translating this would be "a system for sensing spiritual impressions of present sickness."

Byosen is accumulated negative energy present at the site of an illness. The original method of Byosen Reikan Ho, as taught by Sensei Usui, does not exist as it once did. The technique learned these days have heavy Western influence, but it still serves the same purpose. It also differs from the original due to the constant tweaks done by individual healers who have incorporated their detecting disease techniques using Byosen scanning.

The Seven Spiritual Bodies and Their Connection to Reiki

Every practitioner works with and is expected to heal the seven spiritual bodies of each client. This is because disease processes can affect other bodies besides the physical one. The seven bodies every human possesses are:

Ka: This is an energy field resembling the physical body, only larger. Ka is formed and grows before the human body. The energy field of Ka is found an inch or two above the physical body. It's the one Reiki practitioners work with the most.

Pranic Body: This body extends beyond the Ka. It is found several inches above the physical body. It's visible in auric photographs. The human's emotional state heavily determines the size of this body. Working with this body is often difficult, especially with spiritually enlightened individuals. Buddha, for instance, was said to have a pranic body spanning over three miles. How does one work with such an expanse of aura?

Emotional Body: This body is larger than the pranic body and is the bank housing all your emotions. This body could suffer blockages if emotions do not flow smoothly, like when we hold on to grief, anger, envy, or sadness. Its close association with the pranic body makes it hard to know when one ends and the other begins. This is the body practitioners target when there is a disruption in emotional states. The release comes from working with this body that drives clients to tears sometimes.

Mental Body: Slightly higher and more extensive than the emotional body, the mental body is the part of you that holds on to holographic images or memories in space. This is the body you tap into when you view past life regressions, see into the future, or have flashbacks of ancient memories. Since there is no concept of time in the spiritual realm, and we live all our lives simultaneously, this body can help you access past or future lifetimes helped by the akashic records.

Astral Body: This is a delicate sheath slightly larger than the mental body. As the name implies, it is part of the body responsible for astral projections or travel.

Etheric Body: This body works solely in the etheric plane. It is infinite, all-pervading, and massless. The energy housed in this body manifests all that we wish for. When there is a length of time between our creative thoughts and the physical manifestation, it is not because this body is diseased. It is due to the time it takes for the idea to be formed before manifesting in our three-dimensional reality.

Causal Body: This is the most infinite and lightest of the bodies. This body connects us to all the other bodies in the universe.

The Concept of Byosen and the Hibiki Phenomenon

Byosen Reikan Ho is a method used to refer to a scan of the client's energy field to sense disharmony or disease areas. This is done because disease processes cause certain distortions in a client's energy field. These distortions or fluctuations are what cause illness or disease.

Reiki healing is based on the premise that sickness has subtle mental and emotional roots. Each disease process begins as an idea or thought, leading to a distinct energy signature in the etheric body. Byosen Reikan-Ho identifies these energy signatures and these areas within a patient's body most in need of healing. Such sites will provide a baseline of energy information, allowing the practitioner to plan treatment sessions.

Sickness could be anything from a broken bone to stress, anger, tension, unhealthy attachments, and so on. In Japanese terminology, impressions are known as Hibiki. Hibiki is explained as a reverberation, resonance, or echoes containing markers of a client's illness. As humans, we may all share the same anatomy, but our different life experiences have shaped us into what we are today.

These experiences may have shaped us for the better in some ways and worse in others, leaving negative marks on us, which, when ignored, could lead to certain illnesses. The echoes left behind by these marks are what you sense during a Byosen scan, which is done before a Reiki healing session.

Hibiki is the pulsing sensation Reiki practitioners experience in their hands during a Reiki session or a Byosen scan. It alerts you to the sensation of Reiki, stimulating the client's blood vessels and energy fields. These sensations present cause contractions and expansions, identifying areas within the body needing healing or balancing.

Therefore, during a session, Reiki practitioners must be mindful of Hibiki. Irregularities in pulsations such as areas where the pulses resound more strongly or weakly indicate a disease process. During Byosen, you as a practitioner must keep your hands hovering over the diseased area for as long as the Hibiki continues (say one to five minutes) before moving your hands to the next position for healing.

Sometimes during healing sessions, it is possible to mirror the sensations or emotions your clients feel. If they pain in a particular area, you may also feel pain in the palm of your hands, and they have an emotional release, you may find your body and state of mind mimicking that.

As initially taught by Usui Sensei, Reiki focused extensively on the student's ability to develop a feel for distortions or Hibiki in another's energy field. It is an art that seems relatively easy, but it isn't. Back then, Byosen took months, if not years, to become adept at. To date, it requires enormous amounts of patience, discipline, and constant application to master. This can be frustrating if you have a short attention span or are not used to sitting pretty while waiting for things to happen. With time and practice, you will become attuned to others' energy signatures.

The Functions of Byosen Reikan-Ho

- It provides information on diseased areas.

- It creates a healing energy field in the client's body.

- It tells you about the energy frequencies present in your client's physical and subtle body.

- It allows Reiki to flow unimpeded during treatment.

- It keeps practitioners abreast of the client's response to Reiki's healing energy during treatment.

The ability to identify Hibiki and read Byosen greatly benefits the practitioner. Its importance exceeds the scope this text can cover. However, other materials can be read to gain more knowledge of this subject. Note that Byosen is not a diagnostic technique. It is only a method of locating and treating the source of disease.

Before attempting to scan another, it is vital to understand the vibrations present in your energy field. Scanning involves laying ourselves bare in a bid to read another. As a result, sessions have a side effect of merging your energy with that of your client. Like I explained earlier, this can be pleasant or unpleasant. Not understanding your present state before rushing into Byosen leads us to "misread" the client's energy signatures.

Levels of Byosen

Heat: The degree of warmth becomes higher than it usually would. This heat indicates toxin accumulation.

Severe Heat: This heat level is greater than the first and can even cause the practitioner's hands to become sweaty. This indicates a more severe level of toxin accumulation.

Tingling: You can feel this as a pinprick or a sensation of pins and needles. This can also manifest as numbness, buzzing, or a pulling sensation. This shows the highest level of toxin accumulation and signifies an area suffering from inflammation.

Cold: You may feel this as a pulsing, throbbing sensation, or cold feeling in the hands or other extremities. Cold also indicates necrosis, death of an organ, or unresolved emotional issues.

Pain: Results from an increase of energy in an area, a sign there is pressure existing in this area, causing a negative symptom somewhere else in the system. Pain is the highest degree of sensation felt during a scan. The practitioner could feel this pain in just the fingertips or up the entire hand and shoulder levels. It is essential to mention that even with pain, the practitioner should maintain the hand positions required to channel Reiki until the pain subsides or reduces, pointing to a decrease in Hibiki.

Before Conducting Byosen Reikan-Ho

Before Byosen, remove rings, bracelets, or any other jewelry from your wrists and fingers. Ensure good hygiene and refrain from using strongly scented soaps or perfumes on your body or hands as some clients can be sensitive to such smells. Please do not eat any strong-smelling foods or spices like garlic as some patients may find its smell offensive.

Make sure your Reiki room is temperature regulated according to the comfort level of your client. Keep blankets or shawls ready if they feel a bit cold during the treatment since temperature fluctuations are common occurrences during a session.

Each session takes about sixty to ninety minutes to complete, so make sure you and your client wear loose, comfortable clothes. Take a bathroom break before the session begins so you are not interrupted by the call of nature midway into the session.

Communication is very important before Reiki. Be pleasant and friendly. Show empathy and address any feelings of fear, anxiety, or uncertainty in their body language. Answer any questions they might have in detail about the session. Establishing this level of trust helps the client feel more at ease.

Some questions you can ask your client before beginning Byosen include:

- How do you feel today?

- What is your current frame of mind?

- Do you have any health concerns or general health issues?

- Do you have any expectations for this line of treatment?

- What is your sleep routine like?

- Would you call yourself a worrier?

These questions could help point out a specific area for treatment even before Byosen is done. Remember, your role as a practitioner is not to heal but to facilitate or guide others into healing themselves. You are merely supporting your clients on their self-healing journey.

You do not have the right or qualifications as a practitioner to offer a medical diagnosis. In severe medical cases, urge your client to seek advice from a trained medical professional of their choice. Only when they do not have specific medical specialists can you refer one or more that you know.

Beginning Byosen Reikan-Ho

• Ask your client to lie flat on the therapy table on their back with their arms lying loosely by the sides. Their legs must be lying flat on the table, not crossed, as it may interrupt the flow of Reiki.

• Fold your hands in the Gassho or prayer position with thumbs at your heart chakra. Take a deep breath and be grateful for the opportunity to help another and be a conduit for Reiki.

• Silently say an intention for the client's wellbeing and healing. You may say a prayer or an affirmation depending on your mindset and belief system.

• At this stage, you can activate any Reiki symbols if you choose to. Invite the assistance of heavenly beings and past masters. After this, with hands still in the Gassho position, raise them to the third eye, offering a prayer or affirmation stating that your hands be guided to exactly where your client needs Reiki and nowhere else.

• With your client lying down on their backs comfortably on the Reiki table, place your non-dominant hand inches away from their crown chakra. The non-dominant hand is used because it is necessary to use a hand where all your awareness is most rarely concentrated. Using your non-dominant hand allows you to stay more sensitive to differences in your client's vibrational field. Your chosen hand is new territory for your mind to connect with.

• Place your hand and awareness about twelve inches above the patient's crown chakra and move your hand slowly over their head, face, neck, shoulder regions, and down the body. During this scanning period, ensure your hand hovers several inches above the patient's form so your palms and the

Reiki energy moving through you move slowly and with intention down the center of their body and from side to side.

- Continue Byosen until you reach their legs and feet. Remain focused while you search for areas in your body emitting unusual energy frequencies. While you can, these energy changes may manifest as different Byosen levels.

- After sharpening your perception of their body, check their subtle bodies or aura by conducting another scan about six inches or higher from their body. For this, you gently raise and lower your non-dominant hand above their body, running your hands from head to toe in a smooth sweeping motion.

Do this to remove any superficial energy build-up preventing you from reading Hibiki. This sweep also harmonizes your client's energy field or aura. When doing this, pay attention to your hands and mentally note any hot spots of feelings. This way, you can determine Hibiki's exact location within the subtle body while staying alert to any unusual energy emissions.

- After the places requiring treatment are determined, channel Reiki to the affected parts. If there is more than one, it's only natural to start with the most affected and end with the least affected. This way, every part gets Reiki within the allotted time for the session.

Typically, practitioners encounter no more than two or three affected areas. However, extreme cases have over three regions requiring treatment.

Notable Salient Points in Byosen

Typically, when regions requiring treatment have been determined, the practitioner checks the client's subtle bodies requiring treatment. After this, the practitioner channels Reiki to affected areas until energy shifts are detected, indicating healing. It would be best if you remained open to energy signals and information coming through to avoid laxity.

Even after Byosen is complete, scan at intervals to understand energy feedback about their overall response to Reiki. This is done because sometimes, clogs and debris linger after Reiki addresses the main areas needing treatment.

Understand that each client will have a different experience. Some may feel nothing but remember that just because they don't doesn't mean nothing happened. You should not, at any point, be unsure of your ability to channel Reiki. Assume Reiki is a bottle of wine. Does its fundamental form change when poured into a sippy cup compared to a wine glass? Wine is wine. It's the same thing with Reiki. Reiki will flow appropriately in levels required by each client regardless of if you are a beginner or a Reiki master.

Trust in the power of Reiki and continue to scan and treat using different hand placements. Some placements allow Reiki to flow better than others. In cases like this, take a deep breath and visualize Reiki flowing without impediment once again. Be careful not to adopt hand placements that cause feelings of fear, pain, discomfort, or unease. Some of these include touching the throat that may bring about fears of strangulation. In a lot of patients, touching their chest area may seem like an invasion of personal space.

Ending a Session

When you finish scanning and focusing energy for treatment, finish the healing session by doing a final sweep. This sweep clears any form of energetic debris that came about during Reiki. As you sweep the aura, say an intention that the patient's negative energies be transformed into positive ones. You can sweep about three to four times, depending on the time you have left for the session. Sweep over your client's entire body slowly and gently. While your hand hovers, imagine a beam of light coming out of your palms to revitalize their energy and align their chakras, bringing them to a state of wellbeing.

Make sure that your scans and aura sweep ends toward their feet. This helps them stay grounded. When the sweep is complete, raise your hands to the Gassho position and say a final mental prayer to the heavens, divine beings, and past Reiki masters for allowing you to become a suitable channel to bring health to your client. Also, mentally, thank your them for permitting you to conduct Reiki for their highest good.

Wash your hands with cold, running water to cut off the Reiki flow and inform your patient that the session is complete. Quietly tell them to get up when they are ready, as getting up in a rush can be a bit destabilizing. You can offer them a glass of juice or water. Do this because Reiki sessions can be so deeply relaxing that people forget aspects of self-care. Fluids help to further flush out toxins released by the session.

Reiki Contraindications

- It is ill-advised to give Reiki to a person suffering from diabetes mellitus (type 1 diabetes). Such patients take insulin injections, and it may reduce the amount of insulin they require daily.

- Never give Reiki to a patient implanted with a pacemaker, as the energy has the power to alter its rhythm due to its electromagnetic properties.

- Do not give Reiki to people receiving chemotherapy or radiotherapy. Even though it can help reduce the pain that is a part of the cancer treatment process, it also flushes out toxins. In this case, the toxins are the chemotherapeutic drugs or radiation energy that functions as part of the treatment. Flushing them could harm cancer therapy.

- People under anesthesia should not receive Reiki because they are under the influence of drugs that help them sleep through a surgical procedure. Administering treatment can rid the body of this medicine and awaken them during the surgery.

- With a fracture, clients should not receive Reiki until the bone is properly set. It activates the body's natural healing. It may cause the bones to fuse before they are correctly aligned.

- Caution should be exercised when treating epileptic clients as Reiki energy could cause seizures.

- During the first trimester of pregnancy, it is best not to expose the fetus to Reiki as the child is at risk and in the prime of development. Once the first trimester is over, there is no risk of serious complications, and pregnant women may receive treatment.

- Clients with mental illnesses should receive medical clearance before treatment. This warning is especially crucial for schizophrenic clients as symptoms could increase short-term and cause distress.

- Hearing aids should be removed before treatments as Reiki could cause howling or increase sound feedback. They can wear these aids once treatment is complete.

- It is advised that clients on thyroid or blood pressure medication must exercise caution before receiving treatment, as the energy balancing accompanying sessions might alter blood pressure levels and the medicines regulation in the body.

Reiki energy is universal and works for the greater good. However, some situations can be quite sensitive, and a physician must be consulted before scheduling any Reiki treatments.

Chapter Seven: Working with Crystals

Crystals are more than just shiny baubles. Geologically, crystals are minerals occurring naturally in nature. These inorganic substances have specific crystalline geometries or structures. The combination of its chemical elements determines the chemical properties of each stone. There are about three thousand known types of crystals, some naturally occurring in nature and other synthetic.

Naturally occurring crystals are formed by volcanic lava, magma, gases, and sedimentation in salt beds of oceans, lakes, or rivers. In comparison, synthetic crystals are grown in a laboratory.

Crystals have been used since ancient times for ritualistic, magical, and healing practices. These days, they are found everywhere, from quartz in ultrasound machines, electric guitars, microphones, smartwatches, and radios, to silicon crystals used in computer chips, cell phones, and televisions, to the crushed graphite crystals in your favorite pencil. People collect them as decorative stones or for Feng Shui in their living or working spaces, while others grind them to a fine powder for holistic remedies or beauty products.

Distinguishing Between Crystals, Rocks, and Gems

Let's get right to why a stone isn't just a stone. Chemistry teaches that elements are the basic chemical components of the earth. Some elements you wear or use often include silver (Ag), Aluminum (Al), and good old gold (Au).

Two or more elements combine in nature or a lab to form a mineral. For instance, sodium and chlorine from table salt, silicon, and iron form red chalcedony, silicon, and oxygen in varying compositions form clear quartz and chalcedony, and boron and silicon form tourmaline.

A crystal is a defined solid consisting of a repeated pattern of minerals in a fixed order to create a crystalline shape. Such shapes can be cubic, orthorhombic, monoclinic, and so on, depending on the unit cells' symmetry. The thing with crystals is that they are a bit picky about their environment. If the right environmental condition is not in place when the minerals are present, crystals will never form.

A gem is made via organic or mineral matter. Gemstones are rare minerals of the highest and purest quality; sometimes they are crystalline, sometimes not so much; examples are pearl and onyx. Typical gems put a sizable dent in your wallet or credit card, but that's okay because they look beautiful after being cut and professionally polished.

The study of gems is gemology. Not to get nerdy too fast, but gemstones are categorized based on their size, rarity, and hardness. Therefore, we have precious gems like diamonds, sapphire, agate, beryl, jasper, ruby, and emerald, and semi-precious ones like garnet, opal, citrine, amethyst.

Rocks are made solely from aggregates of homogenous minerals and come in different forms. They have no unique mineral or chemical makeup, with their sizes ranging from pebble to mountains.

Common rocks are granite, limestone, basalt, and sandstone. While not all rocks can be cut, polished, and deemed valuable, certain rocks like lapis lazuli, turquoise, azurite are coveted.

Crystals: Bogus or Genius?

The lattice of each crystal comprises atoms and molecules in specific placements. Their molecular arrangement determines their physical and chemical properties. Atoms in science are the nucleus or primary units of energy. The particles in each crystal vibrate or resonate at unique frequencies interpreted by you are qualities or feelings.

Nikola Tesla had stated that the secrets of the universe were cloaked in vibration, energy, and frequency. Years later (in 1905), Albert Einstein provided us with his relativity theory, explaining the relationship between matter and energy. An entire century later, Laurent Lellouch, a French physicist, made calculations based on Einstein's relativity theory to demonstrate mass conversion to energy at a subatomic level.

Marcel Vogel, an IBM scientist, provided the first scientific proof of the power of crystals. He studied crystals under a microscope and observed that they took on the shape of whatever he was thinking about. He concluded this property resulted from the banding and disbanding of the molecules in its structure, allowing them to emit vibrations at a constant frequency. Vogel also observed clear quartz to discover its metaphysical power to store thoughts, like how sound recorders store sound.

Humans, like crystals, are also made up of atoms and molecules. We also vibrate at our frequencies. These frequencies determine our moods, energy levels, or wellbeing. When we are happy, we vibrate at a high frequency, which serves as a "de-stressor" and promotes vitality. When we are sad or ill, we have low vibrations. This is the reason your moods and energy levels, like yawns, are contagious.

When you are close to a specific crystal, its vibrations affect you.

These vibrations could stimulate electrical nerve impulses or channel energy through your energy pathways (chakras). Crystal vibration can also affect cellular, glandular, or tissue metabolism. These vibrations positively impact your mental, physical, and spiritual wellbeing. Each crystal has specific properties for the mind, body, and soul. Some work well on their own, others work better when amplified by other stones, and some stones negate one another when used together. Thus, it is crucial to understand each crystal's properties before attempting to work with them. Little wonder, there is an entire field dedicated to studying the power of crystals, called crystallography. This science alone is the sole winner of 28 Nobel prizes.

The Benefits of Crystals

Listen to Your Gut Feeling: The 21st century has us all trapped, living life like corporate monkeys. Some people live on their desks, with twice daily (or more) caffeine shots to get through the day and not wonder why the clock is so slow. We rely on the mantra, "If it ain't broke, don't fix it." As naturally intuitive individuals, we need to listen to the flashes of insight and our inner voice. Crystals have tremendous power to help us think outside the box. You know when it's time to make a change or leave your corporate hellhole and start something new. You step out of the routine and into your intuitive world, which leads to better things.

Help Increase Your Focus Level: Our brains never totally shut down, except when we sleep. Some folks have found creative ways to bypass that natural process. Crystals can help you focus long enough to meditate, visualize for success, and direct your energies in the direction of your highest benefit.

Dissolve Emotional Blockage: You must have passed through one form of trauma or another. If you haven't, you are riding an impossibly long stroke of luck. Obsidian offers protection from emotional blockage and repressed emotions and healing from addiction.

The moonstone is excellent for soothing emotions. Amazonite offers emotional healing and growth. Carnelian helps with abuse, celestite awakens the beacon of hope, while pink calcite enables you to find love in the middle of despair. Having the right crystals is a sure step to healing and moving forward.

Remove Negative Energy from People and Spaces: Have you ever entered a room where you felt trapped? Like you were spiritually suffocated even when the windows are open? Or maybe you have met someone who feels so off you want to avoid them. That's bad energy in action.

Black tourmaline, selenite, prehnite, apophyllite, clear quartz, violet scapolite, and rainbow fluorite are excellent crystals to get rid of bad vibes and protect you against future negativity. If you find you can't help but keep a messy space, dumortierite and barnacle crystals can help you with better organizational skills.

Increase Energy and Productivity: Some days, you can't help but drag yourself out of bed. Maybe for you, this is an everyday occurrence. Perhaps you are not a morning person, or you can't explain your feelings of lethargy. If you have undergone tests that confirm you are in the prime of health, some crystals can help with enthusiasm and confidence.

Carnelian is better than your usual morning coffee roast. Rubies increase stamina and blood flow. Amethyst helps power you through exhaustion. Bloodstone keeps you far away from elements that prevent you from experiencing positivity.

Create Inner Peace: There must be something you are thinking of right now. That thing has probably stolen your smile, your sleep, and your sense of peace. Whatever it is, hematite, lepidolite, Blue lace agate, Angelite, kambaba jasper, larimar, Mangano calcite, and tree agate are a few crystals you can use to stay grounded, find balance and help you stay calm during the storms of life.

Buying Crystals and Cleansing Them

There are many places to purchase crystals. You can find gems online through a local retailer, metaphysical shops, online auctions, and even airport gift shops. Buying gems in shops is better. This way, you can closely observe them, hold them in the palm of your hand, and see if they resonate with you.

Crystals are like wands. They pick you; you don't pick them. If you buy online, be careful of fake sellers and inauthentic gems at cutthroat prices. Ask questions about if the gemstones have been dyed, irradiated, or coated with petroleum or oil. There are many stories of gemstone dealers trying to pass off fake gems as natural stones.

To clean crystals, you can choose one or more of these options:

- Place them under the full moon for a night or in direct sunlight for not over 15 minutes.

- Pass them through the smoke of cedar, sweetgrass, lavender, or white sage.

- Hold them in your palms and channel Reiki energy to cleanse the stone.

- Place them in a vessel containing ocean water, then rinse off in plain water and air dry.

- Bury in fresh soil or raw organic brown rice. Throw soil or rice away or compost it after use.

- Place crystals on top of flattened selenite, clear quartz, or amethyst for no more than four hours.

- Clean neckpieces with embedded crystals using a damp cloth so you don't deteriorate the string or chain.

Cleaning crystals depends on how often and for how long you work with them, besides the reason you use them. If they are meditation stones, you can cleanse them weekly. If you wear them daily or sleep with them at night, you must clean them daily. The more often you use your crystals, the more attuned to them you will be. This way, you will intuitively know when to clean them.

After cleaning, store them in black or red silk. You could also use a faux velvet cloth or drawstring pouch. For more massive stones, store in display cases or boxes separates from one another to prevent damage.

Never place them near windows because sunlight can damage or dim their appearance. I would advise you to keep them away from small animals and areas where they can manipulate others' energy fields without their consent. Manifestation stones should be kept well out of reach.

Charging Crystals

There are several ways to charge crystals. You can use the full moon, 5 minutes of direct sunlight, seawater, rock salt, clear quartz, solar or lunar eclipse, or burying it in the earth.

This text will only explain how to give them a Reiki boost. Each crystal has its energy, but you can program them with the Cho-Ku-Rei and any Reiki symbols that coincide with your intention. If you are a Reiki master, you may attune the crystal with the master symbol, so it becomes a master crystal.

Crystal Grids

Crystal grids are a group of crystals placed in a set pattern (usually geometric) in a chosen area and programmed with a specific intention. Grids are a method to heighten the power of crystals. Just like a single stone is powerful, using several similar stones or several stones with similar metaphysical qualities will heighten their power in leaps and bounds. The gems you incorporate into a grid depend on availability, choice, and most important, your intention for the grid.

Typically, the center stone should be larger than the rest surrounding it. You can use grids for many reasons. Popular among them are manifestation, cleansing, protection, and healing grids. Your geometric pattern could be in a square, rectangle, hexagon, rhomboid, or a more complex arrangement like a mandala.

Creating a Crystal Grid

• Ensure your crystals are cleansed and charged before you begin.

• Pick your center stone. Your centerpiece is the one with the primary quality you intend to manifest. It could be differently shaped, a different type, or cut from other crystals in the grid.

• Choose your pattern. Regardless of what symmetry you choose, place the crystals equidistant to the center stone. For instance, in a square grid, you use five stones comprising one center stone and four stones at each corner, all placed at an equal distance to the center stone.

• After forming the grid, use your index finger to trace an imaginary line from one cornerstone to the next and from the center crystal to each of the surrounding ones. These lines will form imaginary "spokes" or grid lines of energy.

- Leave the grid in the set position, but remember to cleanse and charge them at least once weekly to renew its power. Repeat steps 1 to 4 after cleansing for the week.

Examples of Crystal Grids

- **Love**: One large rose quartz + rose tourmaline or rhodochrosite and clear quartz (an energy amplifying stone).

- **Abundance:** One large citrine + tiger's eye or aventurine.

- **Harmony and Peace:** One large amethyst + aquamarine or sodalite.

Choosing and Using Crystals in Reiki

There are two primary ways to choose a crystal:

- Intuition

- Intention

When choosing intuitively, you find you are drawn to a particular crystal. Its energies call to you. You pick it up, and it makes you feel something. For instance, when given two emerald rings, you will prefer one stone to the other. Your preference is beyond the cut, polish, and sheer brilliance of the stone.

It's just a gut feeling. I must warn you that when you shop intuitively and pick a crystal, the feeling may not always be good. Sometimes, you could feel out of sorts or sad. There may be unresolved emotional issues the crystals bring up. When these issues are resolved, it goes back to being a feel-good stone.

Trust your intuition to connect you to a stone whose vibrational energy is just the panacea you need. If you choose by intention, it means you have a particular need or challenge you want to be resolved. This could be anything from relationship or money problems to controlling your temper or channeling creativity.

Relationship problems benefit from rose quartz, garnet, and morganite. Tackle money problems with citrine, pyrite, and green aventurine. Calm flaring tempers with a bloodstone, smoky quartz, howlite, peridot, and amethyst. Creativity boosters include carnelian, ametrine, iolite, herkimer diamond, and tangerine quartz, and others.

Not everyone practices crystal Reiki. However, some practitioners combine crystal healing and Reiki to amplify the holistic healing effects and experience. Since each gem possesses a unique energy signature, it is essential to discuss the body's seven energy channels and the crystals that resonate with them.

- **Root Chakra (Red, Black, Brown, and Gray):** Bloodstone, onyx, red jasper, ruby, red garnet, hematite, obsidian, smoky quartz. Associated with high passion energy, good fortune, and staying grounded.

- **Sacral Chakra (Orange):** Moonstone, carnelian, coral, orange calcite. It is associated with acceptance, pleasure, wellbeing.

- **Solar Plexus Chakra (Yellow):** Citrine, topaz, yellow sapphire, amber, Tiger's eye. Associated with strength, vitality, joy, self-confidence, intellect, and self-esteem.

- **Heart Chakra (Green and Pink):** Morganite, moss agate, green jade, rose quartz, watermelon tourmaline, kunzite, emerald, aventurine, pink and green tourmaline, malachite, mica, tiger iron. Associated with joy, inner peace, unconditional love, total acceptance of others.

- **Throat Chakra (Blue):** Sodalite, apatite, turquoise, Angelite, lapis lazuli, aquamarine, amazonite, blue kyanite, chrysocolla, blue lace agate, chalcedony, blue sapphire. Associated with authenticity, wisdom, protection, communication, and loyalty.

- **Brow Chakra (Dark Blue or Indigo):** Tanzanite, lapis lazuli, sodalite, calcite, quartz. Ajna is associated with logic, rationality, communication, focus, and creativity.

- **Crown Chakra (Purple, White, Clear):** Selenite, labradorite, amber, alexandrite, amethyst, clear quartz, alexandrite, fluorite, diamond. The crown chakra is associated with knowledge, divine wisdom, and spiritual awareness.

A lot of crystals used in energy or Reiki healing are pocket friendly. You can find them in crystal balls, wands, or blunt-tipped points. Crystal balls are famous for being the tool of the trade for only fortune-tellers and gypsies. Energy healing is here to disprove that theory. If you come across the crystal you need already encased in a crystal ball, then go for it.

As their name indicates, energy wands are crystals or gems cut and shaped to resemble a tapered stick. Charge these wands with Reiki energy by engraving tiny Reiki symbols on them. This way, you can channel Reiki even more effectively. Some crystals have been shaped to end in sharp points. During Reiki, they are turned away from the client to divert negativity or turned towards the client to enhance positivity.

In Reiki sessions, you can use crystals to complement or amplify Reiki energy. Below are a few ways to do so:

- Keep them at strategic points in the room to heighten Reiki.

- Place them beneath the Reiki table. Energy transfers from the bottom of the table to the room and your client.

- Wear them as jewelry. This way, Reiki is amplified as it passes through you.

- Give them a crystal or two to hold. Depending on your intention for the session, some stones are better held in the dominant hand and others in the non-dominant hand.

- Place them on your client's energy centers to bring about upliftment and comfort.

To understand better how to use crystals in Reiki, you can search for advanced crystal Reiki texts, online courses, or find a book on crystallography.

Chapter Eight: Non-Traditional Reiki Modalities

There are thousands of Reiki modalities today. A lot of texts and websites talk about only twenty. Reiki modalities are also called types, branches, schools, or systems. Don't let the names fool you. They are all the same.

Reiki branches refer to a particular way a master imparts Reiki knowledge, or the specific elements taught by a school or organization. Many Reiki systems are offshoots of Usui Reiki, while others existed long before Mikao Usui. Adding new features to an existing branch makes a whole new one.

Non-Traditional Reiki Branches

Jikiden or Eastern Reiki: These are specific schools of Reiki developed in contemporary India. This form of Reiki incorporates subjects like aura healing, chakra healing, Hindu deities, and many Tibetan and Yoga elements. It does not have influences from Dr. Hayashi. Even though Jikiden and western Reiki both originate from Usui Sensei's Reiki, they are different. Jikiden, like western Reiki, is a spiritual practice used in physical treatment. When a trained Jikiden healer channels the radiating energy, symptoms of ailments such as burns, scrapes, stings, toothaches, and even recovery from surgeries can be alleviated.

Benefits of Jikiden

- It is non-denominational, meaning it does not affect your chosen religion.

- It is non-invasive, gentle, and soothing.

- It helps relieve labor pains and accelerates injury healing.

- Jikiden helps with addictions and all forms of psychological trauma.

Tibetan Reiki: This is another branch of Reiki founded on Usui Reiki's doctrine. Tibetan Reiki was first developed by Iris Ishikuro, a student and cousin of Madam Takata. Iris's membership with the Johrei Fellowship and studies with her sister at a Tibetan temple in Hawaii proved to influence this form of Reiki, a system she called Raku Reiki.

Iris's system was birthed from her dissatisfaction with her cousin's steep rates for third-degree Reiki attunements. For this reason, she made Raku Reiki affordable for all. She trained only two masters: Her daughter Ruby, and Arthur Robertson. Robertson taught Reiki in the '80s and is credited with founding Tibetan Reiki.

There is a belief that Tibet is the secret fountain of all spiritual wisdom and that traditional Reiki is an ancient though forgotten form of Tibetan holistic healing. The arguments for this surpass those against it. Many historians claim that the four original Reiki symbols in Usui Reiki are secret Tibetan mystical symbols. Robertson also mastered Tibetan shamanism and taught it along with Raku Reiki.

Seichim Reiki: Seichim (pronounced say-keem) originates from the ancient Egyptian word sekhem, meaning energy and power or power of powers. This form of Reiki originated from Egypt and was recently rediscovered. Like Usui Reiki, the energy in Seichim is received through the crown chakra and channeled through the hands.

The practice as we know it today started with Patrick Ziegler, an American who visited Egypt in 1970. Ziegler experienced Seichim spontaneously as a swirling blue light shaped like an infinity symbol in Giza's great pyramids, the same place he was initiated. Historians argue that Ziegler relied heavily on Usui Reiki Ryoho in crafting Seichim from practice, symbols to attunements. Only the energies are uniquely different.

Seichim is an old and sacred hands-on healing art form that transforms energy non-invasively. It works with the practitioner's higher consciousness to ensure the wellbeing of both the psychic, physical, and emotional bodies. It preaches harmony, love, balance, and true enlightenment. No matter what the origins of Seichim are, it has its vibrations. This powerful and intuitive form of feminine energy compared to the more masculine Usui Reiki.

The first style of Seichim is close to Usui Reiki, with four attunements in the former as opposed to three in the latter. The second style has Egyptian roots with two facets. Each facet has eleven steps and four levels. The third style has Tibetan roots with three levels.

Ziegler then initiated Tom Seaman, an American originally from Idaho. Together, they encountered a South Indian Seichim master called Marat. He passed down the ancient knowledge of Seichim as transcribed from hieroglyphics by Buddhists of that period and exported to Japan and India.

Shamanic Reiki: Shamanism originates from Saman, a Manchu-Tungus word meaning "one who knows." It is not organized religion or formal ideology but a spiritual practice that incorporates the energy of expanded natural forces and spiritual realities to create harmony for ourselves and others. Reiki and shamanism are individual powerful spiritual healing systems. When combined they are a force to reckon with.

A shaman is an individual who, in an altered state of consciousness, can travel the spirit or other-worldly realms to receive messages and effect changes that manifest on the physical plane. They also possess the ability to retrieve energy, wisdom, and power from other worlds. Shamanic Reiki increases your awareness of oneness with all that exists, aligns you with your highest consciousness, and explores the vibrations unique to you.

This form of Reiki also helps you find your life's path, balances, and measures your energy centers. It also increases your connection to Source, self, and others. All parts of you, be it day to day mental programming, past life experiences, or present-day challenges, all benefit from this Reiki. Shamanic Reiki is well known for soul retrieval — a process where the essence of your being or lost energy is retrieved from another realm and returned to you.

Soul loss is usually suspected when someone feels hollow inside and has lost all hope of living. Issues in the present life may cause this issue, or karmic debt carried over from a previous lifetime. Soul retrieval is a complex process requiring multiple sessions, but it brings a roundabout positive change when complete.

In levels 1 and 2, you are activated as a healer and connected to Source through alignment with our most primitive roots, communicating and connecting with divine guides, helpers, and past masters to call upon the forces of nature for your empowerment, healing, and the wellbeing of others.

Karuna Reiki: The word karuna is a Sanskrit word that means "compassionate action to alleviate others' sufferings." Although a commonplace term in Hinduism and Buddhism, Karuna is the most ancient of Reiki's non-traditional forms. It was built on the foundations of Usui Reiki and formally created in the twentieth century (sometime in 1989) by Marcy Miller, Kathleen Milner, Maria Abraham, Mellie-Ray Marine, and Pat Courtney, and then developed by William Rand.

Rand received Karuna in the form of symbols. He, together with some students, experimented with different attunement processes to match with each sign.

Formerly called Sai Baba Reiki, this Reiki system was developed following a plea to the universe to fill in the gaps left by Usui Reiki. Karuna is shrouded in more mysticism than any other branch or Reiki, and the symbols have multiple functions.

Karuna's vibrations are so high, it links you to ascended masters, angels, and other divine beings. When used together with traditional symbols, your Reiki power is amplified to the nth degree. Karuna Reiki serves many purposes, some of which include:

- Releasing karmic blocks.

- Connecting you to a state of increased consciousness.

- Clearing mental blocks and controls addictions.

- Dissolving self-sabotaging behaviors and unconscious patterns of your shadow self.

- Heightening creativity.

- Helping with healing and building relationships.

- Healing trauma at cellular and subcellular levels.

- Aligning lower chakras.

- Clearing negativity

- Empowering you to achieve goals.

This Reiki course has three attunements, four master symbols, and about eight treatment symbols, each with unique frequencies that bring about hope and healing.

- Karuna I — Zonar, Halu, Harth, Rama.

- Karuna II — Gnosa, Kriya, Iava, Shanti.

- Karuna III— Om, Dumo, Nin Giz-Zida, Dai-Ko-Myo, Raku, Yod E Om-Atma

I have treated most of these symbols in chapter five. Other Reiki systems developed from Karuna Reiki include:

- Tera-Mai Reiki, by Kathleen Milner

- Karuna Ki Reiki + Mudra technique, by Vincent. P. Amador

- Holy Fire Reiki, by William Lee Rand

Angelic Reiki: This is a practice of healing, transformation, and self-care which utilizes the energy of the divine mind. Angelic Reiki is full of new possibilities that change negative situations and the structure of present realities. Its roots go back to the lost continent of Lemuria and Atlantis, where humans and angels lived as one.

This Reiki is not a belief system. Some practitioners would say it defies explanation. The simplest way to explain angelic Reiki to another is that it is a system that allows your highest self to commune with angels to enable the manifestation of divine perfection in the plane you perceive as your reality.

Though simple in structure, it is enveloped in boundless possibilities. Attunements here are unique because energies are transmitted directly from the heavens, unlike other Reiki forms where attunements are "filtered" through the conscious awareness of masters. This process begins a transformation that aligns you with divine perfection.

There are four degrees in two attunement levels. Archangel Metatron leads attunements given by the angelic kingdom of light along with thirty other archangels known as the "Mighty Sarim," and your specific guardian or healing angel. Before this, there is a process known as "karma cutting" overseen by Archangel Michael, a cleansing that provides wholeness to all fragmented pieces within. During the attunement, you receive healing qualities present in the crystals of Atlantis. These symbols are archetypes of the energies of creation. An archetype called Lord Melchizedek grants four ascension activations and blessings at the galactic level.

After this process is complete, you become connected to all seven vibrational levels of divine form. The symbols become anchored and automatically activated, so you experience them on all spiritual levels through sacred geometry. Practitioners of angelic Reiki have their guardian angels assist them during healing sessions.

Kundalini Reiki: This is an effortless, yet powerfully effective spiritual practice intended for self-development and healing that began with Ole Gabrielsen. It is of a higher vibration compared to Usui Reiki and uses no hand positions. It only combines Kundalini energy with Reiki.

In Hindu myths, Kundalini Shakti is the serpentine goddess who embodies the enlivening of all things, including the revelation of divine power (Shakti). She lies asleep at the base of the spine coiled three and a half times around the root chakra.

There are no complex attunements in this Reiki. Three energy activations and six boosters strengthen the chakras, allowing the flow of divine energy that frees you from energy blockages. The cleanse that is part of this Reiki prepares you for the Kundalini awakening. This allows you to connect to vibrational energies possessing frequencies like Kundalini energy.

The Kundalini energy is the power you channel alongside Reiki for physical, spiritual, and etheric healing. Integration into Kundalini Reiki takes seven days, but you are advised to wait a week between each level. In the first level of attunement, the healing channels are open to Kundalini. The crown chakra, Anahata, and hand chakras open and become stronger.

Your body prepares for Kundalini awakening, and you learn to conduct this energy for personal and distance healing. In the second level, there is a partial awakening of Kundalini. The chakras are strengthened, and the main energy channel opens. The opening allows the Kundalini fire to travel from the base to the solar plexus chakra. This process further prepares the body for a complete energy release. You learn a meditation method that increases Kundalini Shakti and channels a higher range of Reiki.

The third level has the solar plexus, base, throat, and sacral chakras are forced open and strengthened. Kundalini Shakti becomes stronger and flows up and out of the crown chakra. You learn how to attune others and crystals. Boosters four to six strengthen your main energy channels to permit higher amounts of Reiki energy (and any other forms of healing energy you have become attuned to) to flow seamlessly.

Benefits of Kundalini Reiki

- Grants you the courage to forge ahead in desperate times.

- Gives you insight into the desires you wish to manifest.

- Helps you heal through acceptance and surrender in tough times.

- Grants you the flexibility of thought to create solutions to seemingly impossible problems.

The Kundalini course is straightforward. The first attunement is personally given. The Reiki master can give second and third attunements remotely ten days after the first. At the end of this process, you automatically have access to crystalline Reiki, birth trauma Reiki, Diamond Reiki, past life Reiki, among others.

Temari Reiki: Jane Stuart Townsend created this Reiki modality. It focuses mainly on the energy centers and is a hands-off way of healing those in need. While studying the delicate art of Japanese flower arrangement called ikebana, Townsend discovered Temari, a Japanese word meaning "hardball" in English.

Using this age-long tradition, she made balls from styrofoam, a material used for many years in technology to heighten radio wave reception when placed on car antennas. She then created a yarn and applique pattern to encase the balls. Each design had colors corresponding to a different chakra.

When creating this Reiki system, she discovered two new chakras: The renal chakra between the root and sacral chakra and the superstructure chakra between Anahata and Vishuddha. Temari Reiki contains elements of traditional Reiki but uses balls as instruments of healing. These balls aid the transmission of Reiki to specific parts of the body suffering from illness.

Townsend believed recovery was incomplete without balls to match the new energy centers. She felt their corresponding organs would be neglected in the session.

Most people who have experienced this form of Reiki confess it feels like a purer, more direct form of Reiki energy. Here is a breakdown of the colors, corresponding chakras, and organs taught in Temari Reiki

> • **Root Chakra (Red):** Bones, rectum, teeth, nails, pelvis, large intestine.

> • **Renal Chakra (Gold/Dark Orange):** Bladder, arterial and venal circulation, kidneys.

> • **Sacral Chakra (Light Green/Orange):** Sex organs.

> • **Solar Plexus Chakra (Purple/Yellow):** Liver, small intestine, gallbladder, colon, spleen, digestive system, autonomic nervous system.

> • **Heart Chakra (Dark Green/Orange):** Lungs, heart, hands, arms, blood circulation to internal organs.

> • **Superstructure Chakra (Dark Blue/Turquoise):** Skull, neck, clavicle, spine, bone marrow, jaw.

> • **Throat Chakra (Dark Blue/Light Blue):** Neck, throat, trachea, esophagus.

- **Third Eye Chakra (Dark Blue/Light Blue)**: Cerebellum of the brain, endocrine system, sinuses, nose, eyes, ears.

- **Crown Chakra (Yellow/Purple)**: Cerebrum of the brain, autonomic nervous system, and cerebral blood flow.

Each Temari session lasts 60 to 90 minutes. Practitioners channel energy to Temari placed on the corresponding energy centers and transmitted Reiki from their hands through the balls to the clients.

Lightarian Reiki: Ascended master Buddha developed this method, which prepares each client for spiritual growth and enlightenment. An increased bandwidth of healing energies extend beyond frequencies Usui Reiki and Karuna can provide with this system. This Reiki is renowned for dissolving unwanted attachments between people, disengaging them from negative energies and experiences, and increasing conscious awareness.

Rainbow Reiki: This was founded in the eighties by Walter Lubeck, author of the bestseller Reiki del Arco Iris, and founder of the Institute of Reiki-Do in Germany in 1980. Lubeck's lineage is Usui-Hayashi-Takata- Furumoto-Brigitte Muller. Rainbow Reiki is a complicated form of holistic healing with karma cleansing elements, astral projection, crystal healing, holistic communication sciences, and healing bodywork. These are all meant to balance out energies via mantras, symbols, chakras, and crystals.

This hands-on therapy is built on the foundation of Usui Reiki. It seeks to expand personal development beyond cultural and individual limits. The most significant difference between this and traditional Reiki is that rainbow Reiki healers delve deeper into physical and psychological ailments through assistance from Buddha and other divine beings for efficient healing.

Lubeck created this modern spiritual pathway from the ancient wisdom of Lemuria. The sessions here are more complicated. They are proven to be more direct and powerful compared to most spiritual healing art forms.

- **1st Degree:** Traditional Usui Reiki, chakra healing and balancing, use of healing oils, aura massages, making rainbow Reiki water, healing animals, babies, and plants

- **2nd Degree:** Additional symbols to strengthen the Ajna chakra. You also learn mental healing, healing of the inner child, and distance healing.

Benefits

- Increased awareness of spirit, chakras, and subtle energy bodies.

- Greater energy levels lasting several days post-session.

- Increased psychic communication abilities, like clairaudience, clairsentience, clairvoyance.

- Purification, expansion, and balance of energy centers.

- Removal of energy blocks that relieve you of physical illness.

Imara Reiki: Two brothers, Geoffrey and Barton Wendel founded this. Imara is a word that means "more." This Reiki invokes Laho Chi's spirit for deep, soul healing. It is a sacred energy form with high vibrations. You must be attuned to the Usui Reiki mastery level to practice. It does not use symbols or attunements to pass on its energy.

Imara is renowned for its effectiveness in healing repressed trauma and past life issues. It works well for distance healing, receiving visions from spiritual realms. To invoke the energy of Imara, chant laho-chi three times. The more the chant, the greater the vibrational energies. Messages or flashes you receive may not always be clear or comprehensive. Keep a journal for flashes or messages you receive. With time, things will make more sense.

Chapter Nine: Receiving Your Second Reiki Attunement

Reiki level two or Okuden is an advanced level where you learn how to harness Reiki through symbols, corresponding mantras, and distance healing. The path to Reiki level two attunement is to first undergo Reiki one training. I advise you to stick to your Reiki level 1 master in your Reiki 2 training, but only if you are happy with them. You must exercise some caution when choosing a master. Some Reiki masters offer Reiki 1 and 2 attunements over a weekend or even a single day. I think that's a bit too much to take in over a short time. Some masters recommend a 21-day purification period after Reiki one, before the second attunement, to bring balance and harmony to the body.

You can find Reiki masters the same way as you would practitioners. Ask family, friends, your physician, masseuse, or chiropractor for recommendations. Check out Reiki circles online on Reddit and Facebook, or search the internet for suggestions. Check the International Association of Reiki Professionals (IARP.org) webpage to meet prospective Reiki masters in your area and familiarize yourself with the code of ethics. This gives you not only an idea of available masters but what to expect from a Reiki course.

Why Study Reiki?

The reasons for choosing this spiritual path are as many as the benefits to be gained. Some are:

- To help a loved one who is gravely ill.

- To supplement your spiritual growth.

- To heal your pet or help in your practice as a veterinarian.

- To begin your Reiki practice.

- To add to your qualifications as a health care practitioner and help in your chosen field of practice.

- To heal yourself of an illness.

Your reasons for learning Reiki may change an hour from now, but whatever the reason is, the teacher you need will depend on your motive for learning Reiki. If you intend to begin a practice of your own, the teacher you choose will differ from the one needed to help you on your journey to spiritual enlightenment. What do you consider when selecting who guides you on your path toward the light?

Choosing a Reiki Master

- **Certification:** In Reiki speak, there are specific qualifications that matter. There are four levels of training. A Reiki Practitioner (RP) is one with second-degree Reiki as his highest qualification. An RP is not qualified to teach but can administer healing to others. A Reiki Master (RM) is one who has completed mastery (third-degree) levels. Further attunements grant you the level of Reiki Master Teacher (RMT). Reiki IV attunements give you the certification of Shinpiden or Reiki Grandmaster. At this level, you are qualified to train anyone from levels 1 to 4, passing on not only tradition but symbols and attunements. Experience is not only measured in years of practice. The amount of interest and commitment matters just as much.

- **Genealogy**: Reiki is a beautiful and powerful practice on its own. Lineage is crucial to some people for learning Reiki. If it matters to you, find a teacher with your desired lineage. Otherwise, do not let this factor impair you from finding a great instructor.

- Different branches have different masters hence slightly different genealogies. You can ask prospective teachers if they can trace their lineage back to the origin of traditional Reiki. The first person in the line must be Mikao Usui, the founder of Usui Reiki-Ryoho.

- **Instinct**: You might be naturally drawn to a practitioner you feel is the right master to help you on your journey. Your reasons may be anything. Maybe you liked their online profile, you have read a book they have written, or you can relate to this person in a way you can't explain.

- **Safety**: You must feel comfortable with your choice of a master. Reiki is a personal journey, so the master you pick matters. They are the ones you permit to help you on this journey and offer advice to you when needed.

- **Charges**: Many people may argue this should top all other reasons. When picking a master, you need to know how fees are paid. Do they accept cash, cheque, or credit cards? Are deposits given in advance, or is the fee paid in full? Are refunds allowed for non-attendance? In many centers, training costs at least $300, paid in full upon registration.

Some masters charge $500 - or more. Some teachers offer scholarships, too, so keep your eyes peeled for that. This charge depends on the additional techniques the master is willing to teach. For instance, some teachers incorporate crystal healing, chakra therapy, shamanism, etc. Note that higher charges do not guarantee a person is a better teacher. Experience counts for something, but only to a certain degree.

Some teachers are natural-born healers who focus more on practice compared to teaching and could possess informal knowledge. If you are new to Reiki, it is a great idea to ask prospective masters what field of Reiki they specialize in and if they have more modalities integrated into their classes.

• **Convenience**: Ask yourself, are you willing to travel miles to learn Reiki? Does your schedule permit such trips? You must seek not only a teacher with whom you feel comfortable but one close enough, so there are no disruptions in your day-to-day life. Would you prefer a class held in person or at a distance (online)? If you are not strapped for cash, you could ask your master to come to you instead.

Always remember you should not be afraid to express your preferences when it comes to learning Reiki. The best journeys happen when you are receptive, engaged, and have faith in the process. This way, you are committed to whatever outcomes arise.

Types of Reiki Classes Available

• **Weekend Classes or Workshops**: These cater to busy professionals without the luxury of time and wish to learn all they can in the shortest possible time frame. The entire three Reiki levels are taught over a weekend or three-day workshop.

• **In-Person Classes**: This class offers the added benefit of being in the same room with the teacher and learning Reiki in a formal classroom setting. You can also watch the teacher perform hands-on training and discuss any difficulties that might arise.

• **Video Classes**: Some masters can teach courses, send materials, and even attunements through videos sent to you personally. The advantage of this form of teaching is that you can watch the videos repeatedly and catch up on any information you may have missed earlier.

- **Extended Classes**: These classes range from a few weeks to several months or years to complete all training levels. The periods between each level allow you to internalize all learned so you can practice one level for some time before moving on to another level.

- **Telephone, Internet, or Long-Distance:** It is possible to attend classes and receive attunements over the phone, via YouTube, or some instant messaging app. The advantage of this form of training is affordable. Some of these classes are even free. The downside is that the quality of training may vary depending on the proficiency of the teacher.

To practice Reiki professionally, traditional in-person classes may be your best bet. It may cause a dent in your wallet, but it's worth it. In-person training helps you with perfect pronunciation of mantras and drawing of symbols with full guidance from a teacher within reach.

Questions You Should Answer Before Deciding to Study Reiki

- Do I have to study Reiki at this time?

- Do I have it in me to commit to the whole nine yards when learning a method of Reiki?

- Can I wait till it yields results?

- What does my gut tell me about prospective master X?

- Are they a good fit for my Reiki journey?

- Would I prefer a male or female teacher?

Questions to Ask Your Prospective Reiki Master

- What has your experience been like teaching Reiki?

- What branch of Reiki is your specialty?

- How long have you been teaching?

- What topics do you cover?

- Do you teach all Reiki levels?

- What are your charges?

- What is your Reiki lineage?

- Can students contact you, outside classes? (Accessibility allows you to gain practical experience outside the class.)

- What can I expect during the attunement process?

- Are there any prerequisites for the course? (Ask this because some masters refuse students who have received their first attunement someplace else.)

- How large is your class? (If you fall under the category of people who find it challenging to learn in large groups, ask this. But if you can get hands-on practice and answers to burning questions you have during the class, this question is unnecessary.)

- Will I get a certificate after the class?

It is highly unlikely that a potential teacher invests over ten minutes of their time answering all questions before you commit to joining a class. If you have a lot of questions, you could meet them up for an informal conversation or ask if you can speak with them over the phone. Always remember to ask if payments for consultation are expected. It is the polite thing to do.

Extended interviews serve no purpose. You or a prospective master can back out if either of you feels there is no rapport. Don't feel bad if a particular teacher refuses you as a student. Just find another. Take your time and consider your options carefully. Be wary of practitioners who claim to "cure" medical conditions and stand against conventional health care!

Preparing for Class

- Practice meditation to connect with your spiritual side.

- Read this book and other texts. Information is power. The more you read, the better you are prepared for your classes.

- Steer clear from illegal substances, alcohol, and tobacco for a week before classes begin.

- Avoid eating heavily to prevent digestive problems that stop you from concentrating.

- Stay away from stimulants like sugar or coffee days before and on the day of class.

- Think carefully about what you want out of the course and set an intention for your future Reiki class.

- Read through any notes or materials provided by your Reiki teacher before class formally starts.

Okuden: The Second Attunement

What does happiness mean to you? A sense of wellbeing? A feeling? An emotion? The opposite of sadness? Your definition will differ from that of the person sitting next to you. Now, attunement isn't happiness, but the analogy is necessary to explain how different people who have experienced it think about it. Most will agree that receiving an attunement is a powerful and spiritual experience, unlike any other.

Reiki attunements were originally called "empowerments" in Japan. After Madam Takata brought Reiki to the West, "empowerments" took on a different name. Some people call it initiation, awakening, transmission, or expansion. They all mean the same thing.

With an attunement, your energy channels are forced open by a Reiki Master, and pure boundless energy can flow through you. Therefore, choosing the master that initiates you into this world is very important. Some students describe this power as one that ripples or tingles from their head to their feet. You are more awake, hyper-aware. Your senses feel sharper than an obsidian blade.

You might ask why an attunement is necessary. After all, this book has all you need. I will answer that question with one of mine. Do you have a right to practice medicine just because you have read a lot of medical books? You need to go to school, pass exams, and get a license. It's the same with Reiki. Read all you want, but you cannot truly practice Reiki until you get an attunement. This process is the key to unlocking all that power (and using it responsibly).

The attunement ceremony used in all Reiki centers is a fusion of the Usui Reiki system and a distinctive Tibetan technique. Since the roots of ancient Reiki are in Tibet, Tibetan techniques forge a stronger bond with Reiki's origins. This addition made under spiritual intuition and guidance has improved the quality of the attunement process, making it more powerful and allowing for a wider range of spiritual energies to be channeled alongside Usui Reiki's usual powers.

Preparing for Your Second Attunement

Your preparation depends on your personal preference and chosen spiritual inclination. Opening your energy meridians is not a joke; whichever way you choose to look at it. The steps aren't set in stone, but there are a few guidelines to help you prepare to connect wholly with your spiritual self before the initiation occurs. These suggestions will help heighten the effects of the attunement process and increase its powers of inner transformation.

Some people choose to renew attunements. While this is their choice, it is not usually necessary. Once you are attuned, you connect to Reiki for life. And like the gift that keeps on giving, you get better and stronger with time and practice. In some traditional classes, attunements are given en-masse, without the students taking some time to prepare their minds and bodies for this life-changing experience.

Studying remotely through video, the internet, or other forms of distance learning helps you learn at your speed. It also gives you some time, ranging from a few days to sometimes a month, to prepare your body and mind for the attunement process before officially receiving it.

Reiki 2 targets your mental and emotional aspects. Because of this, the attunements you gain at this level open your world to a higher vibration that grants you a sharper, keener awareness of yourself and the potential you have for emotional and mental balance.

- Pick a date for your attunement. My advice is that you pick a date relevant to you, like your birthday, anniversary, or some other date that matches an important day in your spiritual path.

- Reduce or stop your intake of animal protein altogether for at least a week before your attunement. Animal protein is tough to digest compared to plant protein. You want your metabolism to be in tip-top shape.

- Do not take alcohol, illegal substances, or smoke for at least three days before.

- Embrace solitude and meditation. Discard all forms of external stimulation such as televisions, radios, and phones.

- Practice self-care. Do this by not undertaking tasks that will stress you out.

- Stay hydrated and sleep well.

- Perform aura cleansing a day before. Doing this clears psychic debris and other people's malicious energy signatures from your energy fields. You can cleanse your aura by taking a bath with sea salt, smudging with white sage or cedarwood. Taking a walk in the rain and using crystals also helps clean your aura.

What to Expect from the Second Attunement

This process is a reconnection or reinforcement to the Reiki energy given in the first attunement. Second attunements are offered in a single time frame, focusing on opening Anahata or the heart chakra. This is because Anahata is a center of both spiritual and physical energy fields. You are asked to keep your eyes closed, not because the attunement is a secret per se, but to heighten your spiritual experience.

Some people have fireworks pop during their attunement ceremony. Others doubt anything even happened. If you fall into the second category, that's okay. The bells and whistles are not a necessary part of this beautiful experience. The period after an attunement is a time of purification and rebirth. This is when your physical body catches up with the higher levels of vibrations you now channel.

Many masters recommend a 21-day purification period to remove energy blocks that prevent you from being the perfect Reiki conduit. This 21-day period is reminiscent of the number of days Sensei Usui spent fasting and meditating on Mount Kurama. At this time, stay hydrated and rest a lot. Some people report having stomach upsets, flu symptoms, head or body aches, and mild fatigue.

These symptoms show the body is going through a mental, emotional, and physical purge. This "spring cleaning" going on may affect your sleep patterns, expose your mind to vivid dreams, out of body experiences, mood swings, changes in thought patterns, and opening of the third eye.

A Reiki self-treatment each day will help you maintain balance if you experience these problems. If you feel stifled by the presence of your family, friends, or roommate, you could check into a hotel for a few days or kindly ask that you do not be disturbed except it is urgent. Solitude is a solace for you at this time of transformation. Please contact your teacher if you have pressing questions.

Chapter Ten: Setting Up Your Reiki Practice

You are done with your second attunement and have taken the plunge and make Reiki a business venture. You started positive of your intentions, but several questions and doubts hold you back. I will attempt to answer some of these questions so you will be well on your way to choosing a business name and logo by the end of this chapter.

Questions to Ask Yourself

- Why is starting a holistic healing practice important?

- What gender or age range do I want to work with?

- What kind of issues do I want to handle and what is the maximum number of patients I can attend weekly?

- What will be the location of my practice, and what will my office hours be?

- How long will sessions last, and how much can I comfortably charge?

- Would I consider getting malpractice or liability insurance?

- What will my cancellation policy be?

- How do I intend to advertise?

- Would I offer discounts or free treatment for the first five clients?

- How will I keep track of patient appointments and payments?

- What are my strengths in practicing Reiki?

- If I work from home, would I be comfortable letting someone into my space?

These questions may seem overwhelming at first, but they require honest answers. They are issues you must consider while branching out. This way, you'll be ready if any unplanned situations arise.

Starting Your Practice

Get Certified: You only need the second attunement to set up shop as a legitimate Reiki practitioner. Consider joining the International Association of Reiki Professionals. Joining a professional association guarantees a lot of benefits, such as:

- Business tools to help you flourish professionally and personally.

- Associations with other prominent practitioners.

- Inclusion in the registered members' directory on the website.

- A membership certificate and includes you as a contributor to classes, conferences, TV programs, magazines, or newspaper articles. These go a long way in helping you advertise your business.

Learn the Legalese: After gaining certification, you must learn of your area's laws about this new practice. Does your state require a license to practice spiritual healing? What are the laws in your country regarding the use of touch or hands-on therapy? Get acquainted with your city hall or the local chamber for commerce for further information.

Helped by IARP and a good lawyer, you can obtain professional liability insurance that covers minor accidents and is affordable. Ensure that clients sign a consent form for energy work. This informs them in print that holistic healing isn't a substitute for professional advice and care.

Practice Makes Perfect: Before getting your feet wet with a legitimate practice, you must have clarity on the workings of Reiki. Experience this energy on a deeper, personal level through self-treatments and treating friends and family members. The more you practice, the better you get at channeling energy. This healing practice takes time to perfect. Thus, your life must be in balance before you attempt to help others.

Choose a Location: You may use Reiki to supplement an existing practice like healthcare or social work. You can also provide Reiki full time or part-time at a center. This cuts off the issue of location. However, if you wish to begin a practice and have no idea where to start and cannot raise capital for a shop of your own, consider working from home. You need to consider zoning laws in your state and if your lease allows the home-based practice.

Working from home saves you money on start-up costs such as rent, property taxes, and commuting. If you don't like home practice, then that's okay. An office space makes your practice look professional and shows people you take your work seriously. An office removes the issues of having a partner as opposed to the idea of working from home and the distractions that come with kids and pets. You will also have to consider if you have a separate room to reorganize for your practice and if your clients can use your bathroom after the session is over.

If you are a female who chooses home practice, for your safety, do not allow male clients into your home when you are alone. Only treat male clients if you have security or people within earshot who can help if needed.

Supplies and Equipment: You will need a massage table and chairs. A lot of Reiki tables are just massage tables repurposed for Reiki. Before picking one, consider if you would prefer to leave it at a spot or if you'd instead carry it from place to place. If your choice is the latter, you are better off with a lighter, portable, yet sturdy table. You also need table accessories such as a carrying case, bolsters, and an attached faceplate.

Use the faceplate for sessions where clients must lay flat on their stomachs. The plate helps keep their face and neck comfortable. You can get good deals on tables online on sites like Etsy and Amazon. You can also ask your local masseuse, Reiki master, or friends. Advert placements for second-hand tables are also seen in classified newspaper ads. Popular brands are Astra-Lite, Earth-Lite, and Strong-Lite. Prices range from 150 to 500 dollars. They also come in different colors and shapes to enhance the client's experience.

Ensure your table has enough legroom for you to put your feet under the back and the front of the table during a session. Practitioners must provide chairs for their comfort and for the patient to sit awhile after the session ends. Pillows and bolsters are also necessary. Chair upholstery must be made of a soft, breathable material. They can be placed under the client's knees to support the spine or under the heads to support the neck.

A sound system is needed to play soothing music that encourages them to relax. It need not be an elaborate set-up. There are royalty-free Reiki tunes you can use. You could buy a CD player. Program each song to last a few minutes so you can change your hand positions at the start of a new song. Lamps, rugs, fresh linen, tissues, healing crystals, and bottled water are some of the equipment you need to personalize your space. Avoid clutter as it is a magnet for negative energy. Do not use scented candles because some people are sensitive to strong odors.

Build a Solid Business Plan: You need to pick a name for your business. Consult a small business analyst and a professional accountant for advice. They will teach you the ropes on the amount to invest, the income to expect, profit margins, and business structure. You are advised on what to do if you decide on sole ownership or limited liability company. Both attract their forms of tax deductions and go a long way in helping you set your financial goals.

Only when you have this figured out can you select a target audience, price plans, bookkeeping strategy, and the decision to have credit card accounts. Set up a single year or 3-year projections. After this, you can decide on a marketing strategy.

Prepare your Marketing Strategy: Spending thousands of dollars on advertising is not a good idea when you are starting. Here are a few ways to get your craft known

> • **Word of Mouth:** Tell a friend to tell a friend. Inform your family, colleagues, friends, and everyone you meet (with a certain degree of tact, of course) that you offer Reiki sessions. You can offer them for free or at a discount to cover running costs.

> • **Business Cards:** Print business cards yourself or ask for the help of a professional. It is an inexpensive way of saying, "Hey, this is what I do and where. I am serious about this." Business cards typically have phone numbers allowing prospective clients to book appointments over the phone. This helps you get a good feel of their energy before they walk in for a session.

- **Flyers:** These are cheaper than business cards. You can explain in a few words what Reiki is, its benefits, where to find you, and your phone number. Stick flyers on notice boards, spas, hospital bulletin boards, health food stores, and New Age book shops.

- **Barter:** Offer a trade of sorts with other alternative therapists like masseuses, Yoga instructors, and the like. They already have an established clientele and often need therapy themselves. Offer to refer clients to them and ask that they extend you the same courtesy. Offer them a business card or flyer just in case.

- **Offer Free Reiki:** Do this when you are in social circles and someone complains of pain. If they are unfamiliar with Reiki, explain to them what it is in a few words: An alternative form of healing that originated from Japan, which has many health benefits, including stress and pain relief. Channel Reiki for 10 to 15 minutes toward the affected area and let them know you offer such services professionally.

Explain how long a session takes and what it is like. Entice them into booking an appointment. Remember, as much as you want your business to grow, focus on helping the person, not fishing for clients. Only if they are interested should you offer them a business card.

- **Wear Reiki:** A hat or t-shirt with Reiki symbols is bound to draw attention. It might start as a compliment to your choice of apparel but quickly graduate into talking about the power of Reiki symbols. If you have the time and it is appropriate, you can offer a sample treatment and ask them to call you to set up a proper session.

- **Write Articles:** You can offer to write weekly, monthly, or quarterly articles for Reiki news or any holistic healing magazine. Write about Reiki or document your Reiki experience. Add your name and number. This form of advertisement improves your reputation as a practitioner. Attend spirit fairs, take a booth with Reiki healers, and offer sample sessions.

- **Website:** Develop a website with the contacts you already have and start an email newsletter to attract more clients and remind the ones you already have of your practice.

- **Volunteering:** Offer your services at a reduced fee at hospitals, drug or alcohol treatment centers, or with a social worker or therapist. Doing this promotes your work and gives you on-the-job experience.

- **Social Media:** Social media marketing is an actual job! Why? Because it's the only way to reach the entire world at the touch of a button. Social media, like Reiki, is energy. Set up a profile online, so your account becomes an extension of you and the energy you put out there. Even though many people carefully curate their media profiles to project a particular image, you can be genuine. Instagram, Facebook, and Telegram groups are ways you can contact others.

- **Pricing Strategy:** Since you have decided on private practice, you will need to determine your fees. Do you want to charge per patient, hour, or session? My best advice is for you to discover what the usual rates are in your area. You can set the same rates as your local massage parlor, although Reiki is priced slightly lower sometimes.

Increase the cost as you become more experienced, gain more knowledge, reputation, and additional skill. Determining your fees can be challenging, but perform a cost-benefit allowance to ensure that you are not underpaid. This way, you have a little leftover to save and cover for expenses.

Many practitioners undercharge of their time and effort due to fear, insecurity, and a lack of abundance mindset. Don't short-change yourself by charging below the bar because you want to grant favors to include everyone. You are afraid that people will ask if your services are worth the buck if you charge too much. Pricing has two levels: Physical and emotional. On the physical level, you tell people what something is worth and put a price on it. On an emotional level, you lay and your worth bare, link it to the services you provide, and you hope people agree with it.

Asking for monetary compensation for your services sends a message to the client that you offer them value for a fee— a trade of sorts, money energy for Reiki energy. If you undercharge, you lose money to sustain your business and yourself. You become unable to pursue your passions. It also implies that you do not value the handwork, time, and energy you put in to offer the services you do.

Charge what you are worth, what is fair, and everything else will fall in place. Holding on to the lack of mindset will not allow a free flow of clientele that value your services. If you are in the business for profit alone, you will have a rough time gaining experience or establishing a client base. Ensure your practice has strong spiritual intentions backed by a need to ensure your client's wellbeing. If you treat clients outside your home or office, ensure they are trusted individuals. Also, stay aware of the taxes that accrue as an independent contractor.

Handling the Competition: Feeling fearful of other Reiki practitioners is a sign that you must address your business plan or do some Reiki self-care on yourself to eliminate fear and lack. Reiki is not a dog-eat-dog field of business. There is enough to go round. Instead of feeling uneasy by other Reiki businesses in your area, understand there is a greater need for healing than you know. It is better to embrace other practitioners with open arms because the intentions you put out there come right back to you.

The strength of your intention and your positive mindset determines the quality of your practice. Once you decide with clarity, determination, and commitment to create a thriving practice, then the universe and higher powers will come to your aid. Lack and the fear of competition are an illusion that goes against everything that Reiki stands for.

This illusion can repel future clients or connections from you. Reiki energy supports harmony and cooperation. It understands that we are all the same. Each practitioner has a place in helping and offering treatment to others. Treat other practitioners as allies, not enemies. You will attract the clients right for you.

Ask for Feedback: Like Ken Blanchard would say, "Feedback is the breakfast of champions." Clear communication is a trademark of professionalism. Keep rhetoric to a minimum, do not assume you know what is best for your client, and don't give unsolicited advice. Documenting client's sessions and asking for feedback goes a long way in improving your practice.

Ask your clients to tell their friends or colleagues their experience in your care. You can also ask them to write a testimonial for you. Having a substantial portfolio of great reviews will serve you better than expensive advertising. Keep detailed session notes, consent forms, and patient-related information. This comes in handy when keeping track of your client's progress in cases of a liability suit and establishing a professional standard for your practice.

Treat your client with the utmost respect and integrity and respect their privacy. Allow them to confide in you, but set time limits for that. Kindly remind them you cannot cross certain boundaries because other professionals are better suited to helping them deal with health or personal problems.

Know when to refer them out and continuously practice self-care, so you are not burnt out. Take care not to prescribe remedies, perform treatments, or suggest medication. You are not a medical professional, and healing is not related to the field of conventional medicine or psychology.

Conclusion

Thank you for choosing this book to educate yourself on the advanced principles of Reiki. I hope you have learned a lot about advanced Reiki, and all the possibilities in this form of energy healing just waiting for you to grab them.

I have treated the different Reiki forms, their symbols and attunements, and compared them to the intricacies of traditional Usui Reiki. Healing begins in the mind, no matter what path you choose. Reiki energy is in abundant supply, and no matter what direction you choose or are drawn to, Reiki will work for you because it is all from the same divine energy source.

Many people learn Reiki for many different reasons. If your motivation is to start a practice of your own, then there are suggestions I would love for you to consider. They are listed in the last chapter. Never forget that Reiki is a journey of healing and harmony. When you channel Reiki to others, you are merely a conduit, a facilitator helping them on their journey to a sense of wellbeing.

If you're just starting and have none of the sensations you're "supposed" to get, understand that they aren't necessary, and just because you don't have those feelings yet doesn't mean your practice is invalid. Remember that it all comes down to your gut and intuition, more than anything else. Also, by accepting that these principles will produce results, it is more than enough to give you the desired outcome. Reiki works, only if you work it. That means constant practice.

Think of it like when you were a toddler mastering handwriting. Your capital letter A probably looked less like an A and more like a deformed pterodactyl eating a pack of flaming Cheetos. That didn't mean what you wrote down wasn't an A, nor did it mean you wouldn't eventually be able to write it down flawlessly without a single thought with enough practice. So, whatever you do, don't quit. Focus less on results and more on the process, and you will not be disappointed.

Use all the tips mentioned in this book to reconnect with your purpose. You can't just read it once and assume you know all you will need to know. Go over it again and again, highlight the bits that stand out to you, and remain a student on the rest of your Reiki journey. Never stop learning. This is how you get better, grow, and improve in your practice.

The masters that existed before you have left their mark on the earth for you to follow. The Reiki precepts and practices will help you when it becomes too dark for you to see. This is the only way you find your path hidden in the shadows- A journey to the remembrance of your most authentic and highest self.

Here's another book by Mari Silva that you might like

Your Free Gift (only available for a limited time)

Thanks for getting this book! If you want to learn more about various spirituality topics, then join Mari Silva's community and get a free guided meditation MP3 for awakening your third eye. This guided meditation mp3 is designed to open and strengthen ones third eye so you can experience a higher state of consciousness. Simply visit the link below the image to get started.

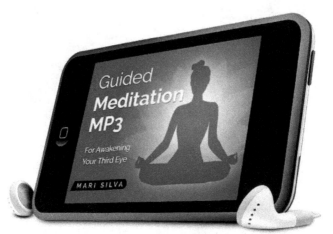

https://spiritualityspot.com/meditation

References

Crystal Crash Course: A Beginner's Guide to Healing Crystals. (n.d.).
Www.Energymuse.com. https://www.energymuse.com/blog/beginners-guide-to-healing-crystals

how to incorporate crystals into your reiki practice ~ kim shipman. (2018, March 14). Yoga Home. https://ouryogahome.com/crystals-reiki/

Inner Essence - History & Types of Reiki. (n.d.). Www.Inneressence.Co.Za. Retrieved from http://www.inneressence.co.za/index.php/reiki/history-types-of-reiki

Kundalini Reiki. (n.d.). Healing Light Energy. Retrieved from https://www.healinglightenergy.ie/kundalini-reiki/

Life, C. (2012, March 5). *Reiki and the Use of Crystals.* Crystal Life. https://www.crystal-life.com/reiki-use-crystals/

Reiki. (2019). Reiki.org. https://www.reiki.org/

Reiki Level 2 Training: What to expect and how to prepare. (2015, September 13). Chakra Meditation Info. https://www.chakrameditationinfo.com/reiki/reiki-healing/reiki-level-2-guide-to-reiki-practice/

Reiki Symbols – What They Are and How They Are Used. (2019, January 24). Karen Harrison. https://www.karenharrison.net/reiki-symbols-what-they-are-how-they-are-used/

ReikiScoop - Grow Through Reiki | To the point, guided information. (n.d.). ReikiScoop. Retrieved from https://reikiscoop.com/

stason.org, S. B. stas (at). (n.d.). *Determine Your True Motive Before Advancing to Reiki Level 2.* Stason.org. Retrieved from https://stason.org/articles/wellbeing/reiki/Determine-Your-True-Motive-Before-Advancing-to-Reiki-Level-2.html

The Ten Dos and Don'ts of Starting Your Own Reiki Practice. (n.d.). The John Harvey Gray Center for Reiki Healing. Retrieved from https://www.learnreiki.org/reiki-articles/starting-your-reiki-practice/

The three pillars of reiki. (2014, August 26). Nature's Pathways. https://naturespathways.com/south-central-wisconsin-edition/september-2014-south-central-wisconsin-edition/the-three-pillars-of-reiki/

Types of Reiki. (n.d.). Medindia. Retrieved from https://www.medindia.net/alternativemedicine/reiki/reiki7.htm

What is Angelic Reiki | Seminars. (n.d.). Www.Angelshouse.Eu. Retrieved from https://www.angelshouse.eu/en/Seminars/What-is-Angelic-Reiki